THE RYE HOUSE

First published in 2018 by Redshank Books

Redshank Books is an imprint of Libri Publishing.

ISBN 978-0-9954834-1-5

A CIP catalogue record for this book is available from The British Library

Design by Helen Taylor

Printed in the UK by Short Run Press

Libri Publishing
Brunel House
Volunteer Way
Faringdon
Oxfordshire
SN7 7YR

Tel: +44 (0)845 873 3837

www.libripublishing.co.uk

THE RYE HOUSE

An Investigative History

Phil Holland

REDSHANK
BOOKS

Lee Valley Regional Park

Rye House Gatehouse is one of many attractions in the 26-mile-long Lee Valley Regional Park.

Stretching for 26 miles from the banks of the River Thames, through north and east London and into Essex and Hertfordshire, Lee Valley Regional Park is a unique leisure, sport and nature destination that attracts more than seven million visits each year.

With popular centres for sport and leisure – including three thriving London 2012 legacy venues available for the public to use, heritage sites such as Rye House Gatehouse, marinas, gardens, riverside trails, relaxing green spaces, campsites, nature reserves and internationally important wildlife habitats – the park is fulfilling its founders' ambition of a 'green lung' for the region and a 'playground for Londoners' with hundreds of great days out for everyone.

Find out more at **www.visitleevalley.org.uk**

DEDICATION

This book is dedicated to my dear mum Daphne Holland whose love of life knew no bounds. She was and will remain always an 'absolute marvel'.

ACKNOWLEDGEMENTS

I would like to thank Alex Farris (Green Spaces Manager for the Lee Valley Regional Park Authority) for his support and Gareth Winn (Senior North Ranger) for his keen interest in this undertaking. When I first approached Gareth with the idea, his enthusiasm was immediate; he too has a passion for the Rye House Gatehouse and its history.

I would like to thank Lawrence Pember, the site ranger, for always being willing to help on the occasions of my forays into the subterranean apartment and for his other assistances.

Finally, my thanks go to the staff at Hertfordshire Archives and Local Studies for their help, the use of their material and assistance with copyright matters.

CONTENTS

INTRODUCTION

This book is the result of a visitor to the Gatehouse asking me for a more detailed history of the Rye House. The leaflet provided was neither informative nor expansive enough to satisfy her curiosity and so she suggested that I wrote one. To which I replied "do you know, I think I shall."

With nearly 600 years of history to research, ambiguous writing, conflicting reports, artistic licence and controversy have been my companions. I have attempted to address any incorrect information so that hopefully a clearer, more accurate account of the history of the Rye House would be the outcome. Where the facts are lost or difficult to determine and thus no definitive answer possible, the topic is instead discussed and considered options derived from the available information are put before the reader.

It is hoped that the ensuing pages will enthuse people about the Gatehouse and the history of the Rye House, and that they in turn will come to treasure the building and recognise its importance as a piece of our country's history.

1. THE BEGINNING

According to Wagner (1891), 'rye' is an Old English term for a common, hence Peckham Rye, and is derived from 'ree', which means watercourse. And indeed, an engraving of nearby Stanstead Bury by C.L.Tyler also includes in its top-left-hand corner an unrecognisable representation of the Rye House, labelled 'The Ree'. Yet in Cotgrave's French dictionary, the word is considered to be of French origin and not English at all; here, 'rie' is defined as an area of waste and untilled or unhusbanded ground. This word is now obsolete in France. This last definition is similar to that of the word 'ri-haela', as found within the Anglo-Saxon Chronicle, which translates as 'rough'. And where Ryhall in Rutland has been called the hall in the rough place, Mills (1991) prefers to describe Ryhall in Leicestershire (Rutland was reinstated as a county on 1 April 1997) as the "Nook of land where Rye is grown." Mills further refers to Rye in Sussex as the "(Place at) the island or dry ground in the marsh"; whereas Gover, Mawer and Stenton (1938) consider that in Hertfordshire, Rye "is from the Middle English phrase atter eye, at the island." From this it is believed that over the years 'atter eye' contracted to 'rye'.

If the appropriate definition is that of an island, then according to Salmon (1728), it has "perhaps retained the ancient name of rye since the time of the Danes when the meadows on both sides of it were covered with water." Rye is mentioned in the Domesday Book of 1086 although it is termed 'EIA' rather than 'Rye', which is considered to be the same place, with Peter (of Valognes) listed as the Lord who held ½ hide from Bishop Odo of Bayeux who was the tenant-in-chief. There are no households listed but there is "Land for ½ plough but it is not there". It further reads: "1 Mill at 3s, from the weirs, 200eels, meadow for ½ plough, from hay 10s. Value of this land 20s when acquired, 10s before 1066, 30s Swein, Earl Harold's man held it, he could sell." This indicates the area's earlier and latest economic value to the king and also that no settlements were present. Not much is known of the area after Domesday Book until on the 7th July 1443, during the reign of Henry VI, when the charter rolls list that Andrew Ogard, knight, John Clyfton, knight,

John Fastoff, knight, William Oldehall, knight, Robert Whityngham, esquire and William Roys were granted a licence to crenellate by the King. This permitted free warren (free hunting of small game); the imparking of the Manor of Rye, otherwise called the Isle of Rye, situated within the parish of Stanstead Abbots; the enclosure of the site of the Manor with stone and mortar and its provision with turrets, battlements and machicolations. Ogard is credited with having had the Rye House built. Indeed, it is his name that first appears on the licence and, moreover, his coat of arms and its supporters displayed in the spandrels either side of the arched entrance. It was also his son who inherited the property, suggesting that the other names or grantees listed were added as a gesture to friends or comrades-in-arms. With its relatively close proximity to Westminster and being suitably designed to display the wealth and status of its owner, the Rye House could offer accommodation for those of the grantees living further afield as well as serve as a hunting lodge when they exercised their right to 'free warren'.

It is curious that the licence allows for the use of stone, given that the Gatehouse is clearly constructed from brick. Suitable stone of good quality was expensive and extremely hard to find in the county, but was this enough to prevent the use of stone for the rest of the house? With thanks to William Worcestre, also known as William Botoner, a traveller and chronicler, it is believed that the remainder of the house, like the Gatehouse, was built in brick. Worcestre visited the Rye House in 1478 and wrote: "the building of the Inner Court with brick and the rooms with the cloister cost" (Harvey, 1969) what is believed to be 2,000 marks and more. Cussans (1870) however preferred 'enclosure' to 'cloister' and indeed from "cum claustro constabat cum" taken from John Hooper Harvey's (1969) edited translation of William Worcestre's Itineraries, from the manuscript in the library of Corpus Christi, Cambridge, which was written in a number of languages, Latin and Middle English (c.1400–1600) being but two, it can, if an alternate translation is used, include 'enclosure'; while "cum claustro consta cum" is interpreted to mean 'When the enclosure consists' (lexilogos.com). Although interestingly, in Clutterbuck (1827) an edited translation by James Nasmith from the same manuscript is included, and 'claustro' isn't followed by 'constabat' instead the wording reads 'cum claustro cum' which translates as, 'When the enclosure', while 'cum claustro' alone translates as 'cloister' (lexilogos.com). Also of interest is the word 'reparacionibus' which is spelt in this fashion by both Nasmith and Harvey but which would seem to have little meaning. However, by replacing the letter c with t, the complete word translates as 'repairs'. So 'cum claustro constabat cum reparationibus' becomes 'with the cloister with the repairs as it was clear' while 'cum claustro cum reparation' becomes 'when enclosure with reparation' (lexilogos.com). A mark incidentally was not a coin but a unit of account. Before the Norman Conquest, a mark was worth 100 pennies. After the Conquest this was raised to 160 pennies 2/3 of a pound or 13 shillings and 4 pennies. Add to this the £1,100 that was the cost of purchasing the Manor of Rye and a further 2,000 marks for the granary, 16 horses, 30 cows and store houses and for the fifteenth century it comes to a princely sum.

That said, it is the purpose of this book to include all that is relevant and controversial to help aid our understanding of the Rye House and its history.

The Rye House has been considered to be of sixteenth-century origin. Indeed, an historian writing in the late-nineteenth century (Winstone, 1889) argued that although the 'licence to crenellate' was granted by Henry VI, the house wasn't built until the reign of Henry VII or even that of Henry VIII. He added that the Wars of the Roses in which landed proprietors were much involved did not allow for any castle to be built. Moreover, the Inventory of the Historical Monuments in Hertfordshire by the Royal Commission on Historical Monuments (England) 1910 also dated the House to the sixteenth century (albeit without supportive argument)!

It's possible that William Worcestre's writings on the Rye House were not readily available to all historians, although both Clutterbuck (1827) and Cussans (1870) were aware of Worcestre's observations as edited by Nasmith. Perhaps Smith (1975) should have the last word. He writes: "The mouldings on the gatehouse contain a number of deep hollows as well as casement mouldings of typically fifteenth-century profile; all these mouldings fit much better into a fifteenth than into a sixteenth-century context. The 1443 date may accordingly be accepted."

The Rye House stood on the left bank of the River Lea very near to its confluence with the River Stort. The Manor is believed to have totalled 156 acres with the land divided up into 50 acres of land, 10 acres of meadow, 80 acres of pasture and 16 acres of woodland. It is further believed that the boundary of their manor extended west to the Lea and east to include the area known as the 'Warren' to a ditch just the other side of where a house stands today. This ditch runs north to south from the Lea to the Stort and in effect creates an island with the area beyond the ditch having "always been called common land" (Andrews, 1902). In 1261, the name 'Insula de la Rye' was used in connection with the area and the Latin 'Insula' translates as island! If then the appropriate definition is used in a literal manner, it suggests there are two islands mentioned within the phrase. Although Andrews (1902) writes 'Insule' which translates as isle, a small island, when quoting from the 'licence to crenellate' from 1443. Hence the "manor of Rye otherwise called the Isle of Rye" (gatehouse-gazetteer) also suggests an island within an island, if of a smaller size. However, Tregelles (1908) states that the "Isle of Rye, on which Rye House stands, is another distinct gravel deposit, and the name denotes an isolated stony ground surrounded by water" which does seem to contradict the above theory. A further ditch that lies in between, just to the east of the present car park, comes off the Lea to the north and divides near the Gatehouse with one arm supplying the moat, while the other continues to the Stort and in essence forms yet another island. Another point of interest concerns the responsibility for maintaining the bridge over the River Lea and keeping a connecting causeway across the meadows for which a toll was charged. The bridge by Tregelles' reckoning was "the most southerly of the cross-valley ways available in all weathers save those by Waltham Abbey and Leabridge." (Tregelles, 1908)

The expertise required to construct such expensive architectural splendour was not readily available in England in the early 1400s. Indeed, the art of brickmaking had only recently been rediscovered – between Roman times and about 1375, brick was used mainly as a minor material. Without any fine corbel work, brick had been used as early as the thirteenth and fourteenth centuries at Little Coggeshall in Essex and East Yorkshire but these were individual examples only: a programme of using brick didn't follow. Whereas after the building of the Rye House, four other nearby buildings were constructed in brick: Hunsdon House, about 1447–8 (although stone was also incorporated); Nether Hall, mid-fifteenth century (Historic England); Hertford Castle gatehouse, mid-fifteenth century; and the Old Palace at Hatfield House, about 1485. In short, it wasn't until the fifteenth century that the use of brick in the hands of skilled Flemish and German craftsmen became a building material of choice in England. Other buildings slightly further afield that were also built extensively in brick include the Manor of the More, near Rickmansworth, Hertfordshire, from 1425 onwards (demolished 1661); Faulkbourne Hall, Essex, 1439; and Someries Castle, Bedfordshire, circa 1448.

There are no records to tell us how the house itself looked in the fifteenth century. William Worcestre's pacings of 1478 do give us the lengths and widths of some areas but alas no detailed description of the buildings themselves. Nevertheless, some writers

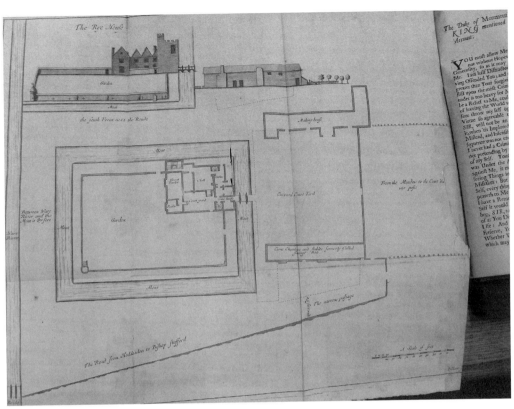

The Plan and Elevation, 1685, drawn up as a consequence of the Rye House Plot.

consider there to be differences and so consequently the house of the seventeenth century (as shown in the Plan and Elevation from 1685, drawn as a consequence of the Rye House Plot, the near-accurate model in the Conspirators' Room and also the equally near-accurate brick markings outlined to the west of the Gatehouse) was not necessarily that of the fifteenth century.

With no definitive description of the fifteenth-century house available, eminent contemporary writers nevertheless offer insightful alternative possibilities to the known house of the seventeenth century. Referring to the Great Parlour[1], T.P. Smith (1975) writes:"Apparently this room was completely independent of the hall-block and may therefore have been a later addition to it." He also writes that by following the 'normal medieval arrangement', where the fireplace in the buttery/pantry backed onto that in the Hall, this was probably instead a doorway. The buttery/pantry was where the butts of wine were stored and measured 22 feet (approx. 6.6m) by 14 feet (approx. 4.2m). It had a newel stair in its north-west angle, a curtain wall with battlements on its east side and (possibly) a store room over it, but with no mention of the newel

1 The Small Parlour is mentioned separately in the following sentence.

stair also supplying access to an upper floor! Smith also suggests that a central brazier heated the Hall (although a fireplace was installed in the first-floor room of the Gatehouse, which is rather at odds with such an archaic form of heating) and that the half-turn staircase, which had landings and a stair-well, to the north of the Great Parlour is not of fifteenth-century origin! J.T. Smith (1993) is of the same opinion with regard to the originality of the staircase, which he interprets as being added by 1683, but unfortunately makes no mention of the theory surrounding the Great Parlour. It's interesting that in Harvey (1969) there's no mention of the parlours as such only the 'rooms'. But if 'rooms' had been translated from the word 'cameris' or 'camera' then 'vaulted ceiling' can also be translated; and with the Inner Court described in the same sentence as being built in brick, would Worcestre instead have been referring to the rib-and-web brick vaulting above the entrance passageway in the Gatehouse? Of further interest: if the seventeenth-century house is again used as an example then from one edition of Sprat (1685) the Plan of the Rye House shows the outside wall of the parlour to be crooked, with the chimney breast of the Great Parlour at its southernmost end in line with the outside wall and yet at its northernmost end it protrudes similar to the chimney breast of the Small Parlour. Similarly, the inside wall of the Great Parlour is crooked as is the dividing wall between the Hall and the Kitchen; but whether any of these misalignments are significant to the theory mentioned earlier, or in general, remains uncertain.

Floor plan, showing the crooked walls and further details not shown on other plans.

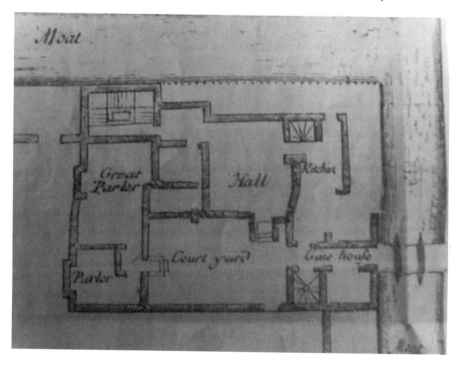

The dimensions of the Hall do differ between authors and are considered by Smith (1992) to be of the correct size for a mediaeval building but overly large for an Elizabethan or later period building. In Harvey's translation, the Hall was measured as 34 feet (approx. 10.3m) long by 24 feet (approx. 7.3m) wide although the original text uses 'pedes', the plural of 'pes', a Roman unit of length measuring 11.6 inches and as such the measurement instead comes to just over 32.5 feet and just over 23 feet respectively. That said, in his translation of Worcestre's writings, as edited by Nasmith, in his *History of Hertfordshire, Vol. 1* (1870), Cussans makes no mention of a hall and instead attributes Worcestre's measurement to that of the Courtyard, which, as we know it, is nearer to 40 feet by 23 feet when taken from east to west. This measurement is taken from the Plan of 1685 and includes the Dividing Chamber (22 feet by 14 feet) between the Hall and the Parlour block. The Latin 'aula', however, can be translated to mean either hall or courtyard, whereas 'aula continet' translates as 'hall contains'. Thus "Aula continet in longitudine. 34 .pedes" (Harvey, 1969) literally translates to 'The length of the Hall contains 34 pedes'. Because 'aula' can be interpreted to mean a courtyard, it's possible to see how Cussans arrived at his conclusion but what isn't quite so understandable is how he overlooked the difference in the two measurements. Unless the Courtyard in the fifteenth century did indeed measure the same as the Hall and the Courtyard was extended at a later date to join with the crooked internal wall.

Cussans also attributes the dimensions given to the 'claustri' – 17.5 yards (approx. 16m) long by 13 yards (approx. 12m) wide – to an enclosure. Dependent upon which Latin dictionary is used, the word 'claustri' has several definitions, cloister and indeed enclosure being but two; but as Cussans translated 'claustro' to mean enclosure later in the text, why he opted for the same translation is puzzling. Unless he considered the enclosure on both occasions to be one and the same, rather like Harvey, but who instead preferred 'cloister'. Moreover, unlike Harvey (who uses the 'yard' as a measurement, which then, as now, equated to 3 feet with 12 inches to a foot) Cussans instead opts for 'rod', which is an exact translation from the Latin 'virga'. The original text uses 'virgas', which if applied when measuring land could be the equivalent of 5.5 yards. This would have made it a structure of some 96.25 yards (approx. 88m) long by 71.5 yards (approx. 65m) which is so far removed from Harvey's translation it's hard to know what to make of either! It is hoped Cussans was referring to an official rod of length that measured 36 inches until the reign of Henry VII (1485-1509) when a measurement of 45 inches was preferred; and indeed the 'tayllors yerd' (45 inches) – tailor's yard – that amounted to 36 inches and a handful – is used separately by Worcestre in the original text when measuring the distance between the Gatehouse and the outer gate (the gate by the ditch): "From the outer gate to the lodge fenced and emparked on both sides is 360 tailors yards" (Harvey, 1969).

Harvey and Cussans differ again, this time over the name of what the former calls the great Court and Cussans the principal Court. Harvey translates the north side as 28 yards (26m) and the east side as 39 yards (36m) whereas Cussans has 28 rods and 39 rods respectively. If the following first proposed area is indeed the great/principal Court then it is 28 yards from the south-east angle of the Gatehouse to the end of the Small Parlour; although if measured from the east Enclosure Wall, then it is approx. 23.5 yards to the end of the Small Parlour with 4.5 yards over! On the east side it is near to 39 yards between the north and south Enclosure Walls although this measurement would include part of the Inner Court as the great/principal Court. Second, it has been assumed that Worcestre considered the north of the House to be facing the same direction as that of today. North actually points from the north-east angle of the Gatehouse (see diagram) and so instead may have opted for north to be looking from the entrance. In which case the distance from, as we know it, the south wall of the Gatehouse to beyond the south Enclosure Wall to the edge of the moat is approximately 28 yards while from the edge of the east arm of the moat and approximately 11 yards (10m) beyond the Small Parlour it is 39 yards. Both of these measurements may or may not be relevant in connection with the Chapel (see below).

As for the Enclosure Wall, the licence to crenellate did allow for the site of the Manor to be enclosed. If it is assumed that an Enclosure Wall was of the same dimensions as shown on the Plan and Elevation of 1685 then it was probably buttressed on its southern side and had cross-shaped loops as a means of protection for the defenders. In addition, there would have been a turret with loopholes in the south-west angle looking to the bridge over the River Lea. It was first thought that this was the only corner to be reinforced but thickenings are shown on the Plan and Elevation in the north-west and south-east angles, while "foundations of three low octagonal turrets found in the 1980s in the corners of the enclosure" (Emery, 2000) indicate that there were earlier turrets at

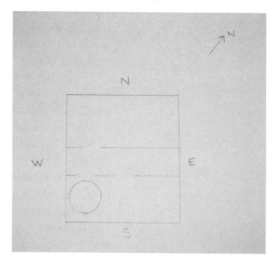

Diagram of the Gatehouse looking from above, with the main entrance at the east and showing the approximate direction of north. (Self-drawn)

these angles also. As to whether the wall had battlements, there is some controversy. The licence to crenellate of 1443 does allow for battlements but the 1685 Plan and Elevation shows the south-west tower but no battlements atop the Enclosure Wall. Conversely, there is a very fortress-like drawing from the nineteenth century showing how the Rye House was believed to have looked in the seventeenth century that has the wall embattled and a turret at the south-east angle. None of this convincingly tells us how the wall looked in the seventeenth century – nor, come to that, how it really looked in the fifteenth century!

Similarly, because Worcestre didn't describe any buildings either to the north or the south of the Outer Courtyard, it is not known for certain what was present there in the fifteenth century. The building to the north included in the 1685 Plan has been described as a barn, but in 1685 it was known as the Maltings and stood approximately on or near to the area of scrub north-east of the Moat. Interestingly, during a geophysical survey (Cromwell, 2016) in which ground-penetrating radar was used on both the Moated Enclosure and the Outer Court, a "much more ephemeral rectangular feature" (Feature A – see photo) was found south of the above building. This finding raises the possibility of another structure, which could simply be from the pleasure-gardens era as an extension to the Maltings – or if the 'feature' is not too fleeting or transitory, as is the way with ephemeral objects, something much more exciting. Harvey calculates that the Outer Courtyard was 155ft (approx. 47m) long and 140ft (approx. 42m) wide. He further calculates these measurements to be 75 and 60 of Worcestre's steppys respectively "a deliberate heel-and-toe measure the length of his two feet which Harvey demonstrated to be about 21–22 inches." (Neale, 2000) The 60 steppys amount to 105–110 feet (approx. 32–33.4m), which is considerably shorter than 140 feet (approx. 42.5m); but by following a northerly direction between the two buildings it is 101.6 feet from the southernmost building to the line of the "ephemeral rectangular feature", which is actually nearer to 58 steppys. Although not exact, this measurement is nevertheless too close to Worcestre's pacings to be ignored – which raises the possibility that the 'feature' measuring about 32 feet (approx. 10m) in length could indeed have

Image from the GPR survey. The survey is lodged with the Historic Environment Record (HER).

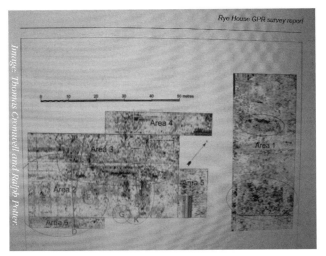

Image: Thomas Cromwell and Ralph Potter.

been a structure, as suggested in the report, but at the time of Worcestre. There's also the possibility that any building was longer than the 'feature' and that equally it fanned out rather like the southernmost building, creating at one end a wider distance in between.

A local historian (Andrews, 1902) was of the opinion that the Retainers' Hall (the Maltings) was the same age as the Gatehouse whereas the RCHM report from 1910 considered the building possibly to be a later structure of the seventeenth century. (Although their opinion with regard to the Gatehouse should be remembered!) The building did have a large fireplace with a seventeenth-century woodwork surround and mostly seventeenth-century and some sixteenth-century panelling on the walls – although it is thought that this was brought in later. (Indeed, an undated and unnamed article states:"the hall has been much altered for the better with fresh pictures, stained glass and remarkably fine old oak panelling.") As mentioned, Harvey also states that the length of the Outer Courtyard is 155 feet (approx. 47m) or 75 steppys which again doesn't tally as 75 steppys equates to 131–137.5 feet (approx. 39–41m). Taking it that the southernmost building or one similar to it was in place in the fifteenth century then it is 75 steppys from the western end of the building to the Outer Wall (embattled or not), which in turn would tie in with Worcestre's measurement of the Moat (see below). To avoid any misunderstanding it should also be mentioned that a 'step' or 'gradus' was a Roman measurement which equated to 2.5 pedes, which amounted to a longer measurement to that of the 'steppy', at very nearly 29 inches.

The southernmost building or "Corne Chambers and Stables" – also formerly called Fallowes Row, Flowings Roe and Slowings Row, but from herein known as Fallowes row – has been described as having had a high pitched roof, and was 25 square feet and 10 feet high at the eaves. In 1685, it had three doors in its south wall, two to the left of centre, as well as two protrusions that were both considered to be chimney stacks with corresponding fireplaces; but whether or not these, or any of the other features, were original is unknown. The earth mound which now exists on this side indicates near to where the building stood with the south-west corner of the building almost in line with the Enclosure Wall. The geophysical survey discovered what "looks to be consistent with a large rectangular structure but its fuzzy nature suggests we may be looking at demolition rubble… instead of intact footings." (Feature B) Interestingly, earlier in 2016 a visitor from the Showmen's Ground reported that he knew the mounds to be made up from rubble which had been deposited there! Nevertheless, the south-west corner of the anomaly is almost in line with the Enclosure Wall.

A chapel served by the "priests, clerks and choristers, of whom there were 16 every day, with four priests at a cost of £100 per year" (Harvey 1969) was also in place. Further from Harvey, Worcestre wrote that Andrew Ogard had a chapel in his house in the last eight years of his life in England. Its exact whereabouts is uncertain, which in turn allows for a number of unsubstantiated conjectural possibilities as to its location. During the geophysical survey, linear markings were found lying in a north-to-south orientation. (Feature K) The approximate measurements are 13 metres by 3 metres and 8 metres by 3 metres, with 3.7 metres in between. The shorter of the two is explained in the geophysical report as perhaps the result of "some later feature or tree throw." These could suggest "an early structure of considerable size" or be "spreads of rubble or similar disturbance" that, as with the explanation given above, were perhaps deposited here in the not-too-distant past. If not, were these the claimed foundations discovered by a Mr William Abel in 1913 when looking for evidence of a tunnel that stretched to Nether Hall? (There is more on this intriguing topic in the chapter 'The Gatehouse and Moated Enclosure'.) With the longest linear marking at 13 metres and both measuring 3 metres at their widest and 3.7 metres in between the two, this does seem excessive for each wall but apparently they do not "behave like solid wall footings." An anomaly to the north of the linear markings looks to be part of the same structure(s) that the geophysical report suggests are the foundations to the conservatory/ballroom. (Feature H) This structure adjoined the west wall of the Gatehouse, whereas the anomaly looks too far south for it to be one and the same. But if the orientation of the linear markings is put aside for one moment and the length of the anomaly is included in a measurement taken from the inside edge of the east arm of the Moat to where the markings fade, the distance is approximately 39 yards (36m). Incidentally, this is the given distance of the east side of the great/principal Court. Alternatively, the measurement from the east Enclosure Wall to the left-hand outside edge of the linear markings is approximately 28 yards (26m), the measurement given for the north side of the great/principal Court. To the right of the anomaly the dark markings are not as numerous, allowing perhaps for the positioning of the Cloister (see below).

Ordinarily, although this was not rigorously adhered to, altars in the fifteenth century were orientated to face east towards Jerusalem ready for the second coming of Christ; but with north at an angle from the front of the Gatehouse, east would have looked towards the recently established park home site of today. It was known for altars to face an east wall, as for example at Ashbury Manor, but at the Rye House the positioning of the buildings would make this impossible and with no other foundations discovered except those outlined earlier, this arrangement or even a direct orientation might only apply to a chapel located elsewhere. Perhaps Cussans' (1870) opinion – that an ancient fore-court once stood upon the bank of the river Lea where the public house now stands – has some relevance here. However, the guide book from 1925 states that the floor of the chapel could still be seen beside the spring that supplied the Moat north of the Enclosure Wall. Unfortunately, this area is on the other side of a fence and is inaccessible. It lies within a nature reserve and is part of an SSSI (Site of Special Scientific Interest). But was this the site of the Chapel? If not, Worcestre wrote that Ogard kept his chapel in his house, though whether this was a literal reference is uncertain – but the fact that no measurements were given, unlike for the Cloister, raises the possibility that the Chapel was indeed inside the House. And furthermore, if no precise orientation of the Chapel was adhered to and Worcestre did indeed take north to face the Maltings, then the front of the Gatehouse faced east. Private chapels were often found in gatehouses and a small chapel or oratory could be part of a room "in which the presence of a fireplace denotes a secular use" (Wood, 1994), a shared use and, in this case – while also bearing in mind the number of personnel, hardly conducive to private prayer – perhaps a separate room at the north end of the first-floor room was used as a bedroom or a study. Alternatively, as stated, altars were known to face walls and so in this case the relevant side of the "linear markings" would have faced east. If however north is taken to be the other given example, then the east side would have faced the road which once again raises the possibility that the wide linear markings are connected with the Chapel. If not, a mediaeval manor house often had a chapel beside it, near to the great hall with a side-room in between. Was the Dividing Chamber the side room with perhaps part of the Parlour block or the same site used as the location for the Chapel?

The Cloister or Enclosure receives scant mention from Worcestre. It's unfortunate that its layout and position are not as well documented as those of Place House, Ware, Hertfordshire, where the galleries of the quadrangle surrounding a garden area are shown to adjoin what are considered to have been the Buttery in the west wing and possibly the Kitchen in the east wing (Smith, 1992). But could the linear markings be the remains of the Cloister? The geophysical report was of the opinion that, when combined with the Chapel, such a large religious complex is more likely to have stood on the site of the public house and indeed the position and the width of the linear markings and the dimensions of the Cloister would appear to make the prospect unlikely. Or do they? Their orientation, irrespective of their position, and the insinuation of a gallery perhaps should not be overlooked. Equally worth considering is that the Latin word 'claustri', as previously mentioned, has several meanings (cloisteryard being another) and the measurement from the east wall to the inside of the right-hand linear marking is very near to, if not exactly, 17.5 yards (approx. 16m)! Consequently, is the inclusion of claustro (or perhaps claustra, a wall or barrier), which Harvey translated as 'cloister' but Cussans translated as 'enclosure', actually in connection with the brick-built Enclosure Wall, which may have been in need of repair, while 'claustri' alone pertains to the Cloister, with perhaps the Chapel adjoining? Or instead, are the linear markings the remains of an outbuilding, a structure often associated with a cloister, maybe lodgings for guests? Smith (1992) is of the opinion that most domestic cloisters were made from timber and probably adjoined the house to the south (Smith, 1993). A drawing by Buckler from 1833 gives a clear view of the south wall of the Gatehouse which shows a row of what look to be indentations, at a height just above the west door arch and giving the impression that a structure had been bonded here. These could have been caused, or perhaps utilised, by such a structure as shown in the drawing by Ellis published in 1806. The lean-to finishes at about where the indentations cease but whether they were made or utilised is hard to determine. However, this raises the possibility that the Cloister was bonded here with the remainder extending to the west beyond the gateway in the Courtyard Wall. Moreover, in an undated and unnamed drawing the indentations are shown to stretch beyond the Enclosure Wall while the Plan (1685) has a gateway in the east Enclosure Wall some 8 yards from the Gatehouse. Smith (1975) refers to Wight's (1972) suggestion that an entrance existed in the south wall of the Gatehouse. This would have been on the Moat side of the Wall and could have served as covered access from the south chamber in the Gatehouse to the garden and the Cloister via the previously mentioned gate. It perhaps seems unlikely that a door allowing entry to the Gatehouse and consequently the rest of the House was located in such a vulnerable position; but if the entrances to the Buttery/Pantry were also in place during the fifteenth century then they too can be considered as equally vulnerable! As can the lower front windows although it was suggested by 'experts' during the 1950s that these were not original, which if true certainly escaped Andrews (1902) who waxed lyrical over their appearance but made no mention of their originality: "On each side of the entrance are two small windows with moulded reveals and heads, and with labels over them which are returned at their ends."

The Moat is thought to date from the time of construction but rather than acting solely as a means of defence was also a statement of wealth and status. Moreover, Smith (1975) writes that the presence of "a drawbridge in front of the gatehouse argues that the inner edge of the moat was originally much closer to the front face than present" whereas in 1685 it certainly was. The drawbridge would have been approximately 11 feet (approximately 3m) long and, when open, rested on a pier. English Heritage in 1992 considered the moat to be nearly 6 metres (approximately 20 ft) across. Interestingly a RCHME report in 2000 stated that the arms vary between 4.0 and 10.0 metres (13ft to 32.5ft), which is very near to William Worcestre's measurement of 20 steppys (which amounts to 35-6 feet or approximately 10.7-11m). This would have extended the Moat near to the west wall of Fallowes Row.

2. THE GATEHOUSE AND MOATED ENCLOSURE – AN EXTENSIVE TOUR

The Gatehouse is all that remains of a fifteenth-century brick-built fortified manor. It is a Grade I listed building and a Scheduled Ancient Monument and as such is protected by law. The Moated Enclosure is considered to be one of the finest examples of the period in Hertfordshire and is part of the Scheduled Ancient Monument.

The Gatehouse is described as being of a 'broad turriform' type and is "one of the earliest, if not the earliest, example of a broad turriform gatehouse to be carried out entirely in brick." (Smith, 1975) Unfortunately, for it to be a broad turriform type, the turret should not be a dominant feature. The turret of today can be

Front of the Rye House Gatehouse. (Photo by the author)

considered as such but, if the various paintings and engravings are
to be believed, the turret of the past was much taller and far more
ornate, as will be discovered later in the text. So, if the Gatehouse
is not an example of a broad turriform type, then what is it? From
those listed in Smith (1975) it is certainly too wide to be a narrow
turriform as the tower would need to be just wider than the entry
passage. This only leaves the great gatehouse type, which has angle
turrets either at all four angles, like that at Nether Hall, or at a single
angle to the front. But with its single turret at the back, the Rye
House Gatehouse would appear not to fall under any of these
categories! Could it be that the turret was positioned at the back to
be closer to the river and the river crossing, which in such an
isolated spot in the fifteenth century, before optical instruments
were perfected, was of more practical use than adhering to a type?

It should also be mentioned that the broad turriform type, with its
cube-like appearance, has separate chambers at either side of the
gateway that carry-up as part of the tower; this also is not the case
at the Gatehouse with its large and open first-floor room! Though
Smith (1975) did hint that separate chambers may once have been
the case at the Gatehouse, which is interesting. The bricks are laid
in the style known as English Bond, although the occasional course
of Flemish Bond is apparent. These styles are easy to differentiate:

Rear of the Rye House
Gatehouse. (Photo by the
author)

English Bond has a course of exclusively either headers or stretchers whereas Flemish Bond has a mixture of both. In the main, each brick is 9 inches long (22.5cm), 4.5 inches wide but only 2 inches (5cm) thick, although some are reported to be 2 1/8 inches thick. It is "likely they were made somewhere in the immediate neighbourhood." (Andrews, 1902) Early brick-built buildings used imported and locally made bricks, but "the methods employed show that much of the ornamental work was done on the spot" (Tregelles, 1908). The 'diaper' work, or the use of blue bricks for the patterning on the outside walls, is created from bricks that are fired at a different temperature because of their position in the clamp kiln used to make them. As a result, such bricks are harder and therefore more able to withstand the elements and the passage of time.

It is believed that the Rye House was built by Flemish, sometimes referred to as Dutch (Ducher), brick-makers working in England at this time who specialised in moulded brickwork. The result is the glorious architecture that has survived to this day. In all, over 50 different types of carved wooden moulds were used and it is the resulting corbel tables, oriel windows and newel stair, as well as the extensive use of brick in its construction, that make the Gatehouse so architecturally important. For example: the front corbel tables beneath the oriel windows are not only cusped within the arches, "they also have cusps to each extrados, forming trefoils

The much-depleted mouchettes. In two of the spandrels, two double-curving blades can be discerned, with a third lower blade also visible in one. In both end spandrels, one half of the trefoil design is also apparent. (Photo by the author)

of mouchettes within the spandrels" (Smith, 1975). For those unfamiliar with these terms, the arches that form the corbel table have arches within them; the outer extremity (the extrados), also has cusps to form three mouchettes that resemble curving daggers within the spandrels (the space between two arches).Although the mouchettes are much depleted, these features not only make the building architecturally important today but, at the time of construction, would have emphasised the wealth and status of the owner. However, such features are by no means unique. Someries Castle, of circa 1448, in Bedfordshire and Faulkbourne Hall, 1439, in Essex also boast similar fine corbel tables, while the latter also has oriel windows which were added in the 1450s.

But with its elaborate brickwork and large windows, was the Gatehouse designed to impress rather than defend? Salmon (1728) considered that the "castle [was] built to awe that neighbourhood." And yet the walls, in places, are over 2 feet (60cm) in thickness, a drawbridge was in place and battlements were atop the tower: all necessary attributes of a domestic gatehouse offering safe haven. In addition, a curtain wall with battlements protected the domestic buildings behind and extended the length of the buttery/kitchen (its remains are still evident). Moreover, its strategic location near to an all-weathers river crossing should also not be overlooked. It would appear from the above that the overall purpose of the Gatehouse was twofold and as such leads to the conclusion that the Gatehouse and indeed the Enclosure Wall were built not only to impress but also to withstand, should the need arise, not a major military offensive but rather the odd minor skirmish. A point perhaps substantiated first by Armitage (1948) who wrote: "and though it is mentioned sometimes as a castle, it does not during any period seem to have been a fortress, yet strong enough perhaps to command a ford here in the river" and Sprat (1685) who wrote: "the garden has high walls so that twenty men might easily defend it for some time against five hundred."

The present north-east arm of the Moat "is a cutting [and] almost certainly not on the old alignment" (RCHME, 2000) that was dug during the restoration works in the 1970s. It is supplied by a stream in its north-east corner and is connected to the Lea by a channel in the north-west corner. Early maps instead show a channel to the south-east of the moat that joined a ditch to run parallel with Rye Road to the public house, where it then headed south to join another ditch.

In 1996, St Albans Museums Service Archaeological Field Unit monitored the replacement of the bridge to the front of the

Slits to the right and left of the corbel table through which the drawbridge chains passed. The dark-coloured wire mesh can also be discerned. (Photo by the author)

Gatehouse and recorded architectural pieces (see below), pot shards and some glass mainly from the nineteenth century. Additionally, in September 2000 the Hertfordshire Archaeological Trust cleared the Moat silts to the south of the bridge for a distance of some 60 feet (approximately 18.46m). No finds of mediaeval material were made and it was considered that previous clearances may have removed deposits of any archaeological value. (For more on the moat, see the chapter 'The Rye House through the Ages'.)

THE TOUR

Above the lime-washed moulded stone Gothic doorway are two slits in the corbelling (a projection from the face of the wall), one on the right, the other on the left of an end arch and each with a wire mesh covering. These are the holes for the drawbridge chains to pass through. On either side of the entrance doors within the rectangular frame are spandrels, which differ in form from those mentioned earlier. Within the spandrels themselves, shapes can be seen beneath the lime wash and, although hard to imagine now, these are Ogard's coat of arms, which includes a star of seven rays with supporters. In the eighteenth-century Oldfield Collection, the star (the shield's 'charge') is represented as having the straight rays

Head of the Gateway at the Rye House Herts:

of a mullet and this is at odds with the wavy or 'estoile' rays on the images found elsewhere in the Gatehouse. The general consensus however, combined with the Oldfield image, suggests that the mullet is the more accurate representation. Andrews (1905) states that it is "a mullet of six points Argent" ('argent' being the heraldic term for silver, although it should be noted that this is frequently represented by white). He also adds that the coat of arms "are so decayed as to be practically undecipherable", which perhaps is why he was unable to see that the charge in the spandrels was a mullet of seven points. As mentioned, Andrews considered the mullet to be argent but although a coat of arms is an individual thing, it can be passed on to one's descendants so it is perhaps pertinent that in the coat of arms of the Danish Gyldenstjernes (his Danish family surname), the charge was or ('or' being the heraldic term for yellow or gold). Interestingly, the illustration of the Head of the Gateway from the Oldfield Collection is also coloured yellow. Additional figures consist of two bird-like creatures, with one that looks to be cowering, if not dead, while on the other side a knightly figure and a dragon face one another and appear to be connected from hand to mouth by a bent implement.

The spandrels from the Oldfield Collection depicting Ogard's coat of arms with supporters and additional figures.

A further point of interest concerns an indentation on the right side of the entrance door a few feet from the ground. On the left side it's also possible to determine where a similar recess once was. These give every indication that at one time they accommodated the handrails of a bridge or bridges that spanned a moat of much wider proportions. The entrance door, incidentally, is of recent manufacture.

On entering the Gatehouse the remarkable sexpartite ribbed vaulting and webs have been partly restored. The webs are load bearing while the ribs have a decorative function. At the rib intersections there are stone bosses repaired with cement.

At the entrance to the south chamber, which has also been called a store room, the bricks on the left and the arch are markedly different from the older bricks to the right. Those to the left and of the arch are the result of restoration work and alterations over the years. For example, it is known that the doorway was wider in 1685 than today. Above is the barrel-vaulted ceiling while on the table by the window are the Victorian architectural pieces found during the archaeological works in 1996, before the installation of the new

The vaulted ceiling above the entrance passageway. (Photo by the author)

bridge. In addition there is at least one older piece, which bears what seems to be a mason's mark. To the left of the table in the wall is a small recess, 9 inches in diameter, where one of the two winding mechanisms for the drawbridge would have been held. The other recess is inaccessible to the visitor, being behind the wooden screen in the north chamber on the other side of the passage.

The door and frame at the entrance to the north chamber, also called the Guard Room in early guide books, were added in the 1980s, like those of the south chamber. To those not of small stature it is hard (probably on the head) not to notice the low doorway. It is mostly thought that buildings such as the Gatehouse had doorways to fit their inhabitants but with the average height of the mediaeval male at 5 feet 7 inches (1.71m) and a female at 5 feet 2 inches (1.58m), this would seem not to be the case. A reason put forward for such low and narrow doorways was to conserve heat but here with such high ceilings the advantage of this must have been limited. The ceiling here is also barrel vaulted while the room itself, certainly in 1685, was divided and had a doorway in the north wall, opposite the existing entrance, which was bricked up in the 1970s. The brickwork surrounding the window has a remaining hinge with other metal work that was probably used in connection with the window shutter, while the chimney breast above the cupboard indicates a later fireplace. At the time of writing, to the front of the room, behind the 'not as old as it looks' wooden screen, sit the conspirators, who can be spied upon by opening the appropriate panels or indeed through the key hole as they plot their execrable deed.

(Note that the subterranean apartment is not open to visitors.)

To the right, at the start of the newel staircase, is the subterranean apartment also known as the dungeon. In the nineteenth century, it was reportedly here that a box of human bones was discovered. This may or may not be true and an open mind should be maintained, although a certain licence with the truth was not unusual in the Pleasure Garden era. A pair of boots with studded soles displayed as being found on a battlefield and described by the guide as being "Hidentical boots what Holiver Cromwell wore" were in fact an old leather pair of considerable length that were previously used in the watercress beds! Even so, it is not inconceivable that in earlier, lawless times some person or persons could have been despatched and then deposited here. Indeed, with regard to the Rye House Plot, Sprat (1685) stated that Richard Rumbold, having heard of Josiah Keeling's treachery, declared he would "knock him on the head", whilst other conspirators had

Diagram of the subterranean apartment. (Self-drawn)

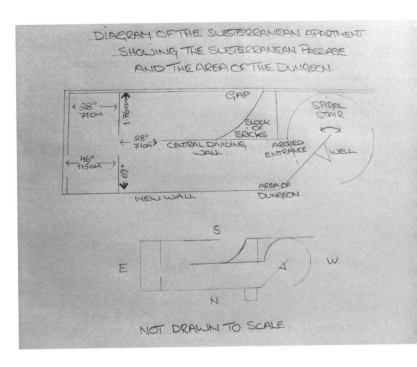

DIAGRAM OF THE SUBTERRANEAN APARTMENT
SHOWING THE SUBTERRANEAN PASSAGE
AND THE AREA OF THE DUNGEON.

GAP

SPIRAL STAIR

BLOCK OF BRICKS

28" 71cm

CENTRAL DIVIDING WALL

ARCHED ENTRANCE

WELL

46" 115cm

NEW WALL

AREA OF DUNGEON

S

E

N

W

NOT DRAWN TO SCALE.

hoped to get him abroad, kill and then bury him. (However, Sprat's testimony cannot be considered as wholly reliable.) Incidentally, after Keeling had informed on the conspirators and had been advised to leave London for his own safety, Rumbold had offered the Rye House as sanctuary; inexplicably, Keeling declined the offer.

The subterranean apartment itself is small, narrow and divided into two sections: one of 9 feet 4 inches (approximately 2.8m) and another measuring 46 inches (approximately 1.17m). It has a width today of 5 feet 9 inches (1.76m) when measuring between the new walls (see below), while the floor of the south chamber above measures 6 feet 8 inches (2.05m) wide and 13 feet 10 inches long (4.25m). The stairs to the subterranean apartment become much narrower and descend again in an anti-clockwise direction to a depth of about 6 feet 9 inches (2.07m). The actual depth is 7 feet 2 inches (2.20m) but there are wooden boards under the cement on the landing which raises the floor a further 5 inches. Andrews (1902) also measured a depth of 6 feet 9 inches but made no mention of a raised floor. Before the arched entrance to the subterranean apartment, the height from the ground to the overhead brickwork measures approximately 5 feet 10 inches (1.79m). To the left by the central pillar is a 2-feet-wide (60cm) opening, some 40 inches (approximately 1m) from the ground, with an aperture that's been plugged with a soft substance. The guide book from 1925 states that at the bottom of the stairs "the visitor passes over a well (now covered in)". This is somewhat puzzling on two counts. First, the top of the well would have been at ground level making access to the remainder of the subterranean apartment precarious. Second, flooding would have been more likely to occur, as it does today. It seems more feasible that the aperture was the well and that what floods the subterranean apartment today is rising water in the well shaft forcing its way in. (It should also be mentioned that any rainfall running down the spiral stair from the open tower also contributes.) Interestingly, the groundwater in July 2017 reached 6 inches above the top of the supposed well.

The way then bears to the right under the arch, where on the other side it is possible for a person measuring 6 feet (1.84m) in height to stand upright, and then heads to the front of the building. The way has a cement surface and gradually rises so that at the far end the space between the floors measures 51 inches (approximately 127cm) and continues to rise until the distance is only 40 inches. This rising floor has the effect of reducing the spread of water in the apartment. On the left of the way is an inner wall constructed from modern materials that sits atop foundations that have a powdery outer layer; but *The Age We Live In*, quoted from Andrews (1902), mentions a "subterranean vault of granite" and indeed an impression of solid foundations is given. A similar modern brick wall on the south side, built in a cavity between the inner and outer walls, supports the pre-cast concrete floor above. Both walls are 9-to-10 inches (22.5–25cm) higher than the older inner walls, which is misleading because, during the restoration of the Gatehouse in the 1970s, a central dividing wall was reduced to the same height as the inner walls to allow the new floor to be laid. The central dividing wall is narrow at one end but has a thick block of red bricks that both reduces its length and widens it on its other side (see diagram). Further it has an outer protective cement-based covering on both sides which hides the bricks beneath from view and a lower protective covering through which brickwork can be seen. Its rounded end, which, in part, is uncovered, is some 28 inches (70cm) from a transverse wall. The base of this wall also has a protective covering while the bricks atop have several missing approximately mid-way along its course. The space between the base of these bricks and the east inner wall is filled with cement and measures 28 inches (71cm). The opening created between the central dividing wall and the transverse wall first steers the individual back on themselves and then, because of a gap in the old inner wall, brings them face to face with the newly built southern inner wall. A further wall of bricks which adjoins the transverse wall and ends by the 'gap' has a reinforced area here. In three previous guide books to the Rye House it is stated that a subterranean passage (tunnel?) once led to Nether Hall, near Roydon, Essex, which is over a mile away and built by the Colt family in the same century as the Rye House. An historian quoted in Andrews (1902) states: "That both Nether Hall and Rye House have a history; and great deeds have probably been done in them, for which their names are noted; and it is quite possible that secret means of communication existed between the two buildings."

However, most historians consider the idea of such a tunnel to be fanciful. Andrews (1902) wrote: "there may (but with no show of probability) have been a subterranean way to Nether Hall or some dungeons or small prison; but nothing of these can now be found." Further, in Andrews another writer is quoted: "It appears from history and the best obtainable information that the valley of the Lea and Stort was more subject to floods formerly than it is now, and therefore any work of this kind though not impossible, was very improbable as along the whole line it would be a tunnel of water." It is also worth considering that Nether Hall lies on the other side of the River Stort and although tunnelling under water was often preferred in case of the need to flood a tunnel, according to the above author this state would have already been attained. Similarly, the present owner of Nether Hall Farm where the ruins are to be found is convinced that the existence of a subterranean passage is a myth. He too considers the ground to have been far too wet for such an undertaking. (These ruins are on private land and not open to the public.)

That said, three pieces of written evidence, contemporary verbal recollections (if somewhat ambiguous) and information from a 1925 guide book on the Rye House all suggest that a short tunnel or subterranean passage did exist in the twentieth century. However, it should be mentioned that the geophysical report of 2016 showed no evidence of a tunnel leading from the southern wall of the Gatehouse. This absence is probably due to depth, as the GPR apparatus was tuned for shallow work to seek out footings and the like.

The first piece of written evidence comes from the *Hertfordshire Countryside* dated May 1970, which contains a letter written by someone who had visited the Gatehouse forty years previously. The letter explained how an old rustic with a torch led his party down the wet and slimy staircase to a small chamber containing the skeleton of a two-headed pig in a glass cabinet. He then proceeded down the secret tunnel, where he came across a well! Said well was covered with an iron plate which apparently sagged when trod

on, giving the feeling that a descent was imminent. (This sounds more like the flooded area at the bottom of the stairs.) At this point, the guide turned off his torch making the girls and women scream (and a few men and boys, I shouldn't wonder!). The guide then led them to the end of the tunnel where all emerged amid dense undergrowth. Unfortunately, the whereabouts of this 'dense undergrowth' is unknown; but an account from a visitor from the Showmen's Ground, where the Pleasure Gardens Fairground used to be, who remembered a tunnel from his childhood within which he used to play, placed the end of the tunnel on the other side of the road in the Showmen's Ground, in line with the south-facing wall! This raises the possibility that the 'dense undergrowth' was located here. Alternatively, the Auction Map from 1881 offers three further possibilities as to the whereabouts of the undergrowth: a strip of vegetation just before the Moat is one option; another between the Moat and a pathway; or yet another between the pathway and the roadway. To add to the uncertainty, two further verbal reminiscences had a tunnel emerging near to the pub, where the last suggested strip of vegetation does indeed extend to, while another had a tunnel heading away from the front of the building
.

The second piece of written testimony is a somewhat jumbled account from an undated publication: "the visitor is permitted to grope his way along a damp, darksome passage, descending a few stairs at the risk of stumbling; and by peeping through a small aperture he will discover a small dungeon, duly lighted by an oil-lamp which serves to display the stalactites which hung from the roof. [The writer is alluding to the skulls that were suspended from the roof.] To this cell there is a massive iron door and inside there is a seat of brickwork running the length of the interior about 8–10ft [approximately 2.4–3.07m], a small door at the opposite extremity of the passage admits us again into daylight." Interestingly, the description 'stalactites' is also to be found in Harper (1904) when describing the "fearsome 'dungeon' affair". He doesn't however make any mention of another exit or a tunnel. This is odd because the *Memories of a Sister...* (1903) contains this: "A winding passage in the rock hung with dripping stalactites… took you to the open air." Equally puzzling is Tristram's (1910) failure to mention another exit or tunnel, although again he alludes to the 'stalactites' and observes that "forms of mediaeval removal are in startling evidence. Their origin may be doubtful but nervous people had better view them after lunch." As a final note on the 'stalactites', Harper adds that they were: "dependent from the roof, and looking superficially at least a thousand years old; but a confidential chat over a glass of ale with an informing stranger reveals the man who made them, and he is not yet a centenarian."

On the whole, with three testimonies describing another exit from the subterranean apartment, such evidence would seem to confirm the existence of a short tunnel or subterranean passage. But was it dug anew as an attraction by the then proprietor, at a comparably recent time, or did it follow an original course? The excavation under the Gatehouse in 1857 discovered "a subterranean apartment with an iron door, having a latticed window" (*Gentleman's Magazine*, 1857, p.711). A year earlier, the guide book stated that a subterranean passage that was supposed to communicate with Nether Hall was "now full of water" and yet no mention is made after the excavation of either an external tunnel or subterranean passage, or of a central dividing wall constituting an internal subterranean passage. If these historically important inclusions had been found then it is hoped that such an esteemed publication of that time would have recognised their consequence and mentioned them accordingly. Similarly, the same can be said for Andrews (1902) who made no mention of a central dividing wall, which, if present and in the same guise as that of today and offering up so many clues, was at least worthy of some recognition; but neither could he find any evidence that suggested a tunnel or passage had ever existed. Although Mr W. Abel, the manager of the Rye House in 1913, was of the opinion that there had been an earlier tunnel to that in use in 1903 because a newspaper article dated the 15th May 1913 stated that he had come across some foundations when trying to locate the underground passage. The article didn't say he'd found any evidence of such and so it is assumed he was unsuccessful, which rather suggests that the twentieth-century tunnel was dug anew. Between 1903 and 1925 there is perhaps further evidence that a tunnel of uncertain length had been in use because a problem with water and foul air had meant it was necessary to brick up the tunnel's entrance – the same entrance, it is assumed, that the central dividing wall to this day shepherds the curious. After 1925 the tunnel was again open to the public and, it would seem, remained accessible after the decline of the Pleasure Gardens in the 1930s.

With regard to the central dividing wall and its origins, an author of romantic novels, George William MacArthur Reynolds, who wrote *The Rye House Plot; or Ruth, the Conspirator's Daughter* and who visited the Rye House in about 1853, is quoted in Armitage (1948) to have observed a 'massive' door at the top of the stairs that led "down into a subterranean passage." In umpteen newspaper articles, though less frequently as time progressed, and independently written guide books from willing expositors from the Pleasure Gardens era, the phrase 'subterranean passage' has been alluded to; but of those perused while undertaking research for this publication, none have described a wall so markedly within the subterranean apartment as that commented upon in the second piece of testimony. In all, it rather suggests that the subterranean passage was the short space between the bottom of the stairs and the arched entrance and that the central dividing wall was fashioned during the twentieth century. Or does it? It follows that, if the subterranean apartment had been explored and developed before 1857, there would have been no need for an excavation. Thereafter, although nothing of the same description with regard to the central dividing wall has been found, two ambiguously written extracts nevertheless cast an element of doubt as to when it was constructed. First, in a description of a visit to Rye House by the Antediluvian Order of Buffaloes in 1873, the writer quotes the guide as saying: "[t]his is the dungeon which was discovered when making a subterranean passage." It does seem odd that a guide should own up to such deceit but perhaps it helps to explain the following quote from a guide book of circa 1898. This states that a subterranean passage had been "partly cleared and explored and can be seen by visitors" but as no reference is made to a dungeon – even though one is mentioned in the *St Pancras and Holborn Journal* in 1872 and in a *Daily Graphic* of 1896, which alludes to the "hideous array of skulls" – it is assumed it was written long before 1898 and transferred from an earlier guide book. Consequently, if the subterranean passage had been only "partly cleared and explored", was the writer predicting there was more to come and that, certainly by 1873, it had arrived in the guise of the central dividing wall? Second, from a *Fishing Gazette* dated 1877: "beneath the Tower is the dungeon with traces of a subterraneous passage said to have formerly existed here." Could this in turn be construed to mean that the central dividing wall was the 'trace' of the subterraneous passage so mentioned?

As to the lay out of the subterranean apartment and how the two elements of an internal subterranean passage and dungeon were incorporated, again material is scant; but perhaps the second piece of testimony is of use here. The author describes the 'seat of brickwork' (the central dividing wall) within the cell complete with 'stalactites', whereas from an earlier description from *The Age We Live In*, August 1873, quoted in Andrews (1902), we find this: "The dungeon in which many a political prisoner has perished and the subterranean vault of granite". Andrews considered the notion of "many a political prisoner" perishing in the dungeon to be "highly mythical" but of more interest perhaps is the author's inference that the dungeon was separate from the vault. The second piece of testimony mentions a small aperture which was peered through to discover a small dungeon while the *Memories of a Sister...* (1903), whose account of the 'stalactites' has already been mentioned, adds this: "in the angle of the wall, was a little iron barred window, showing inside a grim dungeon… revealing a ghostly skeleton". On the cover of the guide book from 1925 is a drawing showing such a window set in the north wall where there is now a new wall (see diagram). The dungeon it would seem was behind this wall.

From what has been discussed so far with regard to the dungeon, its omission from the guide book of 1856, the lack of any reference to it from the excavation of 1857 and Andrews' apparent refusal to recognise the attraction as authentic evidence of an earlier dungeon, it would seem to be an innovation from the latter part of the Pleasure Garden era. Or was it? The guide from 1873 claimed it "was discovered when making a subterranean passage" which if true would mean it pre-dates the Pleasure Garden era. If not true then an attempt to discover the purpose of the original subterranean apartment is necessary. Whether the iron door with a latticed window present in 1857 is the same massive iron door so described in the second piece of testimony or the massive door at the top of the staircase that led down to the subterranean passage described by Reynolds in Armitage (1948) (who visited the Gatehouse in around 1853) is uncertain. An iron door, whether massive or not, does seem to suggest that something needed to be contained or protected, rather like a vault; but as none of the three accounts correspond and each describes its door differently, it's hard to determine if these doors are one and the same. There is a drawing of the massive door, as described by Reynolds, in Armitage (1948), but because of its angle and dark colouring, this gives no clue as to the presence of a latticed window or any certainty as to what material it is made from. It's also possible that the use of the word 'massive' was coincidental because the same word is used by a further author to describe a door in another part of the building (see below). Or does the phrase 'a subterranean apartment with an iron door, having a latticed window' (which doesn't use the word 'massive') suggest that this door was part of the apartment and not separate from it, and thus had been installed to create an enclosed and secure space? But as to when or if this door was installed, or when the door at the top of the stairs was installed, all remains unknown.

The newel stair is exceptional in that, from the subterranean apartment going up, it's made entirely from brick and is one of the earliest examples in the country; moreover, at 3 feet 1 inch (approximately 90cm), it is also unusually wide. Understandably, many of the bricks which now make up the treads are of recent manufacture and over twenty have a protective covering of cement;

but those bricks at the bottom of each step, in the main, do look of an age. When the staircase was built it would have taken a great deal of timber to create the formwork for the vaulting which was necessary to support the individual bricks of the treads. Ordinarily, steps were made from stone and of one piece because this was cheaper and because the skill required was not as considerable or as demanding. Other nearby properties that have an early brick-built newel stair, dated from the period 1400–50, are Someries Castle, Bedfordshire, and Faulkbourne Hall, Essex. Sadly, at nearby Nether Hall, mid-fifteenth century (Historic England), the handrail and newel stair have fallen - or as this has been reported, 'sunk'.

The newel stair and handrail with the main part of the brick treads covered. (Photo by the author)

The spiral stair ascends in a clockwise direction. A reason given for this is one of defence should the Gatehouse have come under attack, in one of those minor skirmishes mentioned earlier. A right-handed swordsman fighting his way up the stairs would have had a hard time of it with the newel (central pillar) as an obstruction. Not so the defenders, who, if right handed, had more room in which to use their swords with effect. In the fifteenth century, however, there were more anti-clockwise newels than before, until by the early sixteenth century anti-clockwise newels had become, if not the norm, certainly more usual. The inbuilt handrail is another very interesting feature in that it is made from moulded bricks. This is a very effective and extremely skilled use of brick which fortunately, for the most part, has remained intact.

If there are 54 steps to the turret, there are only 23 to the first-floor room. This room has been known as the Conspirators' Room although, according to Armitage (1948), this title is "fanciful" and there is no existing evidence to prove that any plotters ever met here. (There is more on this subject in the chapter 'The Rye House Plot'.) This is all rather unfortunate, as would be the eerie popular beliefs or folklore associated with the room if experienced alone on dark night. Hayllar (1948) expands upon the cynical explanations given by Andrews (1902) to these beliefs by adding that the "mysterious murmurings and whisperings" were noise from nearby trees. Both mentioned insect activity in connection with the walls being "full of warning tickings" while both dismissed the "creaking stair" as non-existent. Indeed, this does appear to be a misnomer, but perhaps the section plan in Andrews (1902) could be of help here. This plan shows the extension added to the north wall of the Gatehouse (see the chapter 'The Rye House through the Ages') with a staircase adjacent to the north wall; so perhaps this was the 'creaking' stair.

The fireplace measures 6 feet 7 inches (approximately 2.02m) wide and only 3 feet 6 inches (1.07m) high but looks functional and is an improvement on the brazier-in-the-middle-of-the-room set-up. With the window shutters closed, the holes for which can only be found on the south-wall window ledge, and a fire blazing in the

The wide fireplace for accommodating logs. (Photo by the author)

The interior of the first-floor room showing the protected rendered wall in between the oriel windows and the weathered remains of a carving. (Photo by the author)

hearth it's not hard to imagine the room, or perhaps part of it, as being comfortable. The wall's rendering would have added to the warmth of the room and was an expensive addition; the remains of this are protected by Perspex and probably date back to the Tudor period. Three iron hinges for the shutters are to be found by both oriel windows while on the window ledge looking east is the weathered remains of a carving that once adorned the exterior of the Gatehouse. The present tiled floor replaced a tile mosaic

The small modern door and the large recess in the South wall. To the right of the door is more protected rendering while the treads of the spiral stair have modern bricks atop with more aged bricks underneath. (Photo by the author)

removed in the early 1970s beneath which was an original tiled floor (Smith, 1975).

The main door in the first-floor room is another subject for controversy. Andrews (1902) believed that the doorway had been enlarged at some stage because the moulded handrail "does not finish rightly at either side of it." However Smith (1975) is of the opinion that the holes that held the hinge-pintles and also the large recess in the south wall give ample reasons to suppose that a doorway of some size has always been present here. What is certain is that the existing door, added in 1985–6, is not of the same size as that mentioned in a guide to the Gatehouse from the middle of the nineteenth century, which described the then door as "massive". To look at the existing door and at the door jamb where there are the remains of a door fastening and bolting mechanism, and again at the large recess in the south wall, it's quite easy to see just how massive the door would have been.

The doorway in the north-west corner was a means of communicating with the rooms over the kitchen. Another writer is more expansive in his description and considered this doorway to be the entrance to the prison from the then aptly named Warder's room, and also a means of communicating with the inhabited part of the house, via a long corridor. It's possible that at some time this room, or part of it, may have been used in this capacity but it was more usual for prisons to be within the gatehouse rather than within earshot of the hall. As a further accolade, the room has also been known as Queen Elizabeth's Chamber. For more on this topic see the chapter 'The Rye House through the Ages'.

Lastly, the centre piece of the room is the model of the Rye House. The Plan and Elevation (1685) drawn up as a consequence of the

The Estate Model

The estate model of the Rye House in the first-floor room. (Rye House Gatehouse, Lee Valley Regional Park)

Rye House Plot is a limited representation of the Rye House in the seventeenth century and the model is based upon this. Smith (1993) is further of the opinion that by 1683 an upper floor and gabled attics had been inserted, the hall had been divided into two rooms and the buttery/pantry converted into a kitchen. The Plan shows the southern aspect of the House only but also gives a floor plan of the buildings located in the north-eastern angle of the Enclosure Wall. The given dimensions are as follows: the Gatehouse, 27 feet 5 inches by 25 feet 5 inches; the Kitchen, 22 feet by 14 inches (approximately 6.76m x 4.30m); the Hall (see the chapter 'From the Beginning'); the dividing Chamber, 22 feet by 14 feet (approximately 6.76m by 4.30m) plus a smaller chamber projecting to the north; the Great Parlour, 35 feet by 20 feet (approximately 10.76m x 6.15m) plus the open well staircase; and the Small Parlour, 17 feet by 16 feet (approximately 5.23m x 4.92m). The Plan depicts the Hall with a doorway to the far right of centre; two gables and part of a third by the kitchen; and three windows on the first floor and one on the ground floor. A wider gable positioned over the Parlour block has a small window near the roof with windows on the ground and first floors overlooking the garden. The model has two windows on the ground and upper floors of the Hall and a window apiece on the upper and ground floors of the Parlour

The triangular block that once had an embedded spike, where reputedly Sir Thomas Armstrong's and Richard Rumbold's heads were impaled. (Photo by the author)

block but not in the gable! Further inaccuracies include the chimney being taller than the turret while the Maltings is positioned too far south. There's a further discrepancy as to whether a drawbridge by this date was still in use. Smith (1975) states that by as early as 1683 there was no drawbridge whereas Armitage (1948) holds the opposite view! The Plan and Elevation from 1685, however, shows a complete crossing with what is more likely to be a bridge.

It is another 31 steps to the turret. Before reaching the viewing platform, a gate (grille) is passed that leads to the battlements. It was reportedly through here that the heads of Sir Thomas Armstrong and, later, Richard Rumbold were carried, as mentioned in the chapter, 'The Rye House Plot'. The triangular block from which the spike protruded that was used to impale the heads can be seen quite clearly from here .

From the viewing platform, a good view of the surrounding area can still be attained and on a clear day London can be seen – the Shard being a popular landmark. But with little to hamper the onlooker, the view in the fifteenth century must have been incalculable to the isolated household. The Plan and Elevation from 1685, looking from the south, shows a much taller and embattled turret with no sign of the chimney, while most of the later drawings, up to the end of the eighteenth century, also show a much taller and more ornate turret than that of today, although not embattled. Above the existing stone coping was an arcade or arched brickwork, atop which was yet more stone coping. Yet more brickwork surmounted this, which the various later drawings show in a gradual state of deterioration; and indeed, in his watercolour 'A View of the Gatehouse' painted in 1793, Turner includes an ornate and slightly ruinous taller turret. In 1795, however, a drawing published in the *Lady's Magazine* shows the turret with an arcade but with no ruinous brickwork above; whereas a drawing by Ellis published in 1806 shows the turret with no arcade and in a similar condition to that of today. Likewise, in his Hertfordshire Sketch Book, Luppino, a scenery painter at Covent Garden Opera House at the end of the eighteenth century, shows the turret in a similar condition to that depicted by Ellis. An engraving by S. Rawle published in 1805 and a drawing by J.C. Smith published in 1807, however, both show the turret in a pre-1795 condition with an arcade and ruinous brickwork above; though Smith's turret is in a better condition than Rawle's. Andrews (1902) states that by "1795 the brickwork above the arcade on the gateway tower was gone". If he is correct, this confirms that both of the latter images were drawn some years before their published date.

The RYE HOUSE, Herts.
Published by Jno.ᵉ Robins & Sons 57 Tooley Street.

Drawn by Ellis & Engraved by A.Warren.   In D. Hughson's Description of London

Engraved by John Rye, From a Drawing by J.C.Smith.   For the Beauties of &c.

THE RYE HOUSE,
Hertfordshire.

London, Published by Vernon, Hood, & Sharpe, Poultry, Nov.ʳ 5,1807.

Top left: Ellis's drawing showing a much reduced turret, 1806. This drawing is referred to again later in the book.

Above: Rawle's engraving of 1805 showing a taller turret than that drawn by Ellis but shorter than that drawn by Smith. This engraving is referred to again later in the book.

Bottom left: Smith's drawing showing a taller turret, 1807. This drawing is referred to again later in the book.

The date of the 11.5 foot (approximately 3.53m) restored barley-twist chimney shaft has also been brought into question; but the considered opinion is that the similar bricks and "deep mouldings argue an early date" (Smith, 1975) and so are compatible with the building, whereas a lighter twist usually denotes a later date. The deep spiral effect of the chimney was attained by a process called 'hewing'. This involved a system of 'cutting and rubbing' the fired bricks to produce a variety of shapes using a brick axe, a hammer and chisel, and various abrasives. The cut-and-rubbed method was favoured over the option of firing the bricks in wooden moulds for a number of reasons but in the main because the bricks were liable to warp during the firing process and also because their complex shape with its "deep undercutting made their removal from the timber mould box... virtually impossible." (Lynch, Watt and Colston, 2006) In addition, the skill of the 'hewers' – usually a 'Ducher' or a 'Flemying' – meant that once the bricks had been fired slowly at a low temperature (800–950 degrees centigrade), they were still malleable and could be cut and rubbed quickly and accurately, then used like building stones to create an impressive chimney shaft. Incidentally, the Gatehouse chimney shaft is the oldest in Hertfordshire.

The barley-twist chimney. (Photo by the author)

By looking west and then at the right-hand corner of the stone coping, a groove marking out a rectangular shape can be discerned. It is here that the earlier-dated carving now in the first-floor room is believed to have once been positioned.

On leaving the Gatehouse and turning right and right again, the south wall of the Gatehouse can be seen to have a large arch-shaped pattern of different-coloured modern bricks (below the left air brick in the subterranean apartment was the entrance to the

The arched pattern in the south wall. (Photo by the author)

tunnel or subterranean passage). As mentioned in the chapter 'From the Beginning', it is considered by one writer (Wight, 1972) that the arch-shaped pattern was once an entrance. If so, the bricks used to block the doorway may have weakened and deteriorated over the years creating the unsightly hole of the 1950s. Another writer (Smith, 1975) disagrees with the entrance theory and believes instead that the south wall was damaged when the enclosure wall itself was demolished. This is also a possibility because the line of the wall, as marked by the foundation bricks, is just to the side of the arched pattern. That said, the Tithe Map from 1840 and the Ordnance Survey Maps from 1880 and into the twentieth century show a protrusion at the south-west angle of the Gatehouse near to or at the damaged area, which may also have been a factor or contributed to the weakening of the wall. Or maybe the wall was severely weakened when the tunnel entrance was created. As to when the Enclosure Wall was demolished, it is difficult to be precise but drawings and illustrations from 1777, 1806, 1823 and 1825 show no wall. The drawing from 1823, incidentally, was supposedly 'taken on the spot' for the *Bon Bouche* publication. Two illustrations by J.C. Buckler from 1826 and 1832 show a wall in each, of differing appearance, south of the Gatehouse with both depicted as being nearer to the Moat than the original. The following year a further illustration by the same artist who'd positioned himself to the south west of the Gatehouse, adjacent to the southern arm of the Moat, shows an open aspect but no sign of a wall at all. From the early twentieth century, a small section of flat-topped wall leading from the south-west angle of the Gatehouse was in place.

Higher up on the clunch string-course, two comparatively normal images peer down from up high. These were added in a relatively recent time and are in variance with the existing grotesques and gargoyles. The male carving is adorned with a ruff and the possibility that these are of Joyce Frankland and her husband William Frankland has been considered; but as there is no mention of any such recognition in a recent written history of the Newport Free Grammar School (which was founded by Joyce Frankland) this possibility would seem unlikely. It would also seem unlikely that one or both of these are replica replacements as Smith (1975) mentions the gargoyles at the south-east and south-west angles with a further "two spaced along the string" and Oldfield's eighteenth-century image of the Gatehouse also shows two gargoyles in between. One of these, it would seem, still remains although an undated drawing does show three carvings between the angles with visages of an unspecified appearance or function.

Both the gargoyles and the grotesques are positioned to ward off evil spirits but there is a distinction between the two: gargoyles have a water-spout to throw water clear of buildings. Gargoyles are fantastical human or animal carvings while a grotesque, although equally of animal or human form, is often depicted with a humorous expression and can also be interweaved with flowers and foliage. The remaining gargoyle at the north-east angle and the grotesques are spread out on the string-course around the Gatehouse. The stone coping on the tower has further grotesques; by moving to the west side of the Gatehouse, the replacement carving to that in the first-floor room can be found, which again is more akin to a normal human visage than that of a grotesque. Also, the "projection which is the back of the fireplace and the flue" (Smith, 1975) can be seen here, a feature that, when combined with the supporting corbel table of cusped arches, perhaps confirms that the fireplace is original.

To the south and to the west of the Gatehouse near each inner edge of the Moat are two Grade II listed remains: first, a fragment of wall with jambs, sill and part head of a window; and second a fragment of wall with jambs and sill of a window. Where these architectural features originate from and when they were made are controversial.

One opinion is that they probably date from the original house of circa 1443 and were repositioned as part of Henry Teale's Pleasure Gardens (RCHME, 2000). Although laudable, this theory overlooks the fact that when the old house (excluding the Gatehouse) was demolished at the end of the seventeenth century (Smith, 1993), the rebuild is depicted through the work of various artists to be of a very different architecture! That is not to dismiss the possibility that the windows were somewhere incorporated into the rebuild; but if not, where had the remains been until the middle of the nineteenth century?

With that question in mind, it has been suggested they are pseudo Gothic windows, made for the Pleasure Garden. This theory is also laudable because a photograph from 1959 shows the south-east window as a complete arch, but the fact that the rebates (grooves which hold the glass in place) are present appears to make them practical rather than just ornamental. Unless of course they were put together using older materials. That said, the sills also have rebates but are very much worn, while they both have holes for iron supports. On the first there are three sets of two, on the other, two sets of two. Again, unless they are part of an amalgamation, these inclusions together with the rebates would seem to add far too much detail for items made simply to be ornaments. If then they are of an age and taking it that they are original features, maybe they were part of the Chapel. This is feasible if the Chapel was elsewhere other than the Gatehouse but again, where had the ruins been? If the Chapel was located on the northern side of the moat beside the stream, as the guide book from 1925 claims, then they may have come from its ruin and been repositioned in the nineteenth century. Alternatively, they could have been brought in by Mr Teale and positioned. This was the case with the old east window of Cheshunt Church, which was placed by the river in the Hotel gardens. This is interesting because at a similar location the plan from the auction sales of 1881 shows a path leading approximately to where the ruins beside the west arm of the Moat are today. Of the other ruin, the photograph from 1959 showing a complete arch is the earliest reference to it observed.

At the south-west entrance, two Grade II listed chimney shafts, included in the scheduling, masquerade as gateposts. They were used as such during the Pleasure Gardens era and had ornamental metalwork hanging from their columns. The 'Monument Details' (RCHME, 2000) suggest that they are: "Probably architectural features from Rye House c1443 repositioned c1868 by Henry Teale as part of his public pleasure garden." The definition of 'circa' is about, approximately, and the word usually precedes a date. Smith

(1992) has dated the barley-twist chimney on the Gatehouse as the oldest in Hertfordshire and so a date preceding 1443 isn't appropriate here. English Heritage, however, in a document from 1992 before it merged with the RCHME, omitted the year and instead dated them as late medieval, which does allow for more flexibility; but if they are of such an age and once thought to have been part of the fabric, how is the lack of enthusiasm from past authors explained? The self-produced guide books on the Rye House make no mention of their historic associations with the house; only the Gatehouse chimney is lauded. Equally unenthusiastic have been the contributions from early or later authors who, although they may mention the Gatehouse chimney, have made no reference of any significance to its companions. Andrews (1902) would seem to consider them as impostors when enthusing about the Gatehouse chimney when he writes: "On the west wall is left the only one of the beautiful Tudor chimney shafts, which must in the early time of the castle have made the building a highly ornamental one" – albeit he did refer to the Rye House as a castle and thought the chimney to be of Tudor origin! Nevertheless, they received no mention.

The chimneys on the rebuilt Rye House as represented by artists

The chimney–gateposts. Note the lighter twists of the chimneys. (Photo by the author)

are very plain and rectangular – there's not a twist in sight. It could be argued that the same could be said for the seventeenth-century house as depicted in the Plan and Elevation 1685: the chimney shafts look very unremarkable, with only the caps indicating a circular shaft while, in some copies, the shafts appear to have edges to them. With matters unresolved, their structure is of equal interest. Given what has been discussed and the lighter twists of the chimneys, it would appear that they are of a later date than the Gatehouse chimney; although unlike most examples from the Tudor period, each has a cap not much wider than the chimney itself. Nevertheless, it's perhaps not surprising that the points raised above have fuelled the theory that the chimneys, although of an age, were not a part of the Rye House but instead brought in from elsewhere.

The north side of the Gatehouse has featured greatly in its history over the years. When the original house was demolished, the rebuild was added to this wall. When this too was demolished, the extension with battlements was added, although this was not properly bonded.

The remains of the Curtain Wall have two openings for windows but whether or not these are original is uncertain. Indeed, in Hooper's 1784 drawing it's hard to determine any openings at all, whereas in Smith's (1807) both are shown and in Buckler's (1832) only the upper is shown. There are also remnants of a brick barrelled vault from the kitchen, of an indeterminate age, that can be seen on the inside of the wall just below the lower reinforced-concrete stitch. The Plan of 1685 shows an entrance to the kitchen at its northern end and from the Curtain Wall, very near in fact to where the lower window is positioned. Gateways in the Enclosure Wall allowing access to the garden area and/or the Moat were positioned near to the House on the northern side – as denoted by a gap in the foundation bricks that mark out the Wall – and approximately 22 feet (approximately 6.76m) to the south of the Gatehouse on the eastern side. This last gateway has previously been mentioned in connection with the Cloister but the originality of any of these features remains uncertain.

As well as the differences between the Plan and Elevation (1685) and the Model, there are also differences between the plans depicted in the three early editions of Sprat's *A True Account...* and the platform brick foundations. In the Plan from the second and third editions, the walls are drawn straight; another dated 1685 shows crooked walls between the kitchen and the Hall, and the outside wall of the Parlour block and the inside wall of the Great

Parlour. Also shown are the doorways opposite the northernmost fireplace of the Great Parlour that allowed access to the rest of the House via the Dividing Chamber, which itself has a further dividing wall here. As mentioned, the Plan gives a date of 1685, the same year as its publication in Sprat's *A True Account...* but as there were two editions that year it is assumed to be from the first edition. These differences are puzzling. And so unless the 'crooked walls' are the result of an inaccurate drawing or of some major alterations that occurred in between Sprat's publications, which would seem unlikely, then the missing 'crooked walls' will remain a puzzle. But if indeed neither explanation is the case then Emery's (2000) somewhat ambiguous account that in the 1980s "the platform site was excavated and the house foundations marked out on the ground" might only confound the mystery. As expected the brick foundations have straight lines and also omit the other inclusions mentioned from the first edition's plan and differ further by having the south wall of the Hall bonded at the corner of the Gatehouse instead of the farther south position as shown on the other plans.

The Gatehouse and Moated Enclosure are all that remain of a once very impressive fortified manor. The fact that they've survived is due in part to their having been of use over the centuries. From private residence to workhouse, museum and public pleasure garden, all these uses were reasons for preservation. That's not to say there were no periods of neglect, as the chapter 'The Rye House through the Ages' will show. Indeed, as a newspaper article from the middle of the nineteenth century put it: the "upper part of the turret has fallen in and the building is rapidly crumbling away... The foundations of the house appear everywhere sapped and the whole must soon fall". This must have been written soon after Teale leased the Gatehouse because the writer adds: "inside is covered with layers of whitewash except the staircase... not a vestige of ornament remains." Fast forward to the 1970s, the Gatehouse was yet again crumbling and the moat slowly choking to death. An organisation with the vision and the necessary resources was needed to restore them both, not to the glory of yester year but certainly to a condition where their history can live.

3. THE RYE HOUSE THROUGH THE AGES

Andrew Ogard was of Danish birth, his real name being Anders Pedersen Gyldenstjerne, and it is thought that the majority of his wealth came from plunder acquired during the Hundred Years' War between England and France. From the Seconda Patent ac Anno II Regis Henrici Sexti M. 13, Andrews (1902) translates "Dacus factus est indigena" to mean that Ogard "was a Dane not exactly naturalized, but denizenised". Other accounts take the opposite view and indeed 'indigena' translates as 'native'. However, at this time, whether a person had been denizenised or naturalised was unclear as both words were interchangeable: it wasn't until later that the status of denizen, which originates from the monarch (or the executive), and native, which originates from legislature by an act of Parliament, became distinct. In any case, according to Shaw and King (1911) this was the only distinction between the two because a denizen's rights and privileges, which had always been at the discretion of the monarch, could be more or less favourable than those of a native. This perhaps first explains the Patent Letter of denization granted to Ogard in 1433 by an Act of Parliament and why, as a denizen, he was allowed to become chamberlain to the Duke of Bedford in 1435 and the MP for Norfolk during the 1440s, as well as to hold numerous offices. In 1438 he became ambassador to the King of France and between 1442 and 1450 was a councillor to the Duke of York. In 1450 he was appointed Vassal of the castle and town of Caen but in July of that year was forced to surrender to the French who were rapidly reclaiming lands lost in Normandy during the Hundred Years' War. Because of this, he lost favour with King Henry but in 1452 was restored to favour and became the Commissioner of the Peace in Hertfordshire and, in 1453, was made Constable of Wisbech Castle. The same Letter of denization listed in the Rolls of Parliament (Vol. IV, p.439) also helps with another matter: there remains some dispute as to when he was dubbed a knight. Dates as early as 1424 or as late as 1442 have been suggested but from the letter in the year 1433, Andrew Ogard is described as a "humble Chivaler" which translates as "humble knight". Which is of some help at least.

Not bad for a soldier of fortune who, along with his Manor of Rye, also held Thele Manor, Newgates Manor, Hayleigh Manor and Thele, Amwell, Hoddesdon and Ware (Andrews, 1902). This extensive list is by no means complete nor does it include his lands in France, the income from which contributed to his wealth. Ogard died at Buckenham, Norfolk in 1454 and was buried by the high altar at Wymondham Abbey as directed in his will.

Of the other grantees mentioned in the licence to crenellate, Sir John de Clifton, 1394–1447 was a Knight of Buckenham castle and Ogard's father-in-law. Sir John Fastoff, or Fastolf, (1380–1459) served under Henry V and was present at the siege of Harfleur in 1415. He was invalided home and so missed the Battle of Agincourt (also in 1415) but returned to assist with the defence of Harfleur in the winter of 1415–16. He was the Duke of Bedford's Master of the Household and also a Knight of the Garter. During the Battle of Patay in 1429 he was accused of cowardice and it took him 13 years to clear his name. Shakespeare used the name Falstaff for one of his comic characters, a cowardly knight in *Henry IV, Part I*; although the spelling is not an exact match, there is a similarity. The imaginary name of John Falstaff was not Shakespeare's original choice. Instead, he'd chosen the name of an actual historical figure, John Oldcastle, a Lollard and real-life friend of King Henry V who was executed in 1417 for leading a rebellion against the king. Objections from the family caused Shakespeare to change the name to John Falstaff. Fastoff died in 1459 whereas the character of Falstaff died as an aged man in Shakespeare's Henry V, which suggests that the character was made up from a mixture of different people, Robert Greene included. As for the other grantees, William Oldehall (d.1460), was a soldier and the Speaker in the House of Commons. He also built Hunsdon House in 1447, a castellated manor house using red brick. Robert Whityngham Esq. was most probably the Sir Robert Whityngham who owned Pendley Manor in Tring Herts and fought on the Lancastrian side during the Wars of the Roses at the battles of St Albans in 1455 and 1461. He also fought at Wakefield in 1460 and Towton in 1461, and was killed at the Battle of Tewkesbury in 1471. About the last of the grantees, William Roys, no information can be found.

Upon Ogard's death, his son Henry inherited the Rye House but as a minor, at about four years of age, he was too young to inherit. The custody of Ogard's heir and possessions was, at one time, granted to Lawrence Bishop of Durham and later, in 1463, the Manor of Rye was granted to George Duke of Clarence where it would seem the Crown held the estate as trustee. Upon Henry's death, the Manor went to his heir, Andrew.

THE RYE HOUSE THROUGH THE AGES

Andrew was a cousin to Thomas Parr who leased the Rye House in 1517, moving there with his wife Maud (née Green), friend and lady-in-waiting to Katherine of Aragon, and his children: eldest daughter Catherine, who was five at the time, William and Anne, the youngest. On 11th November of that year, Thomas Parr died of the sweating sickness at his London home in Blackfriars. He was 40 years of age. Maud, at 25, was left to raise her children. She established a schoolroom and appointed a single tutor to educate them alongside several of their cousins. It is not impossible that the first-floor room in the Gatehouse was used for this end, though this is speculation. It was away from the main house and certainly big enough in its present form to accommodate a number of children. The association the immediate Parr family had with the Rye House lasted until 1531 when Maud died and Anne, at the age of sixteen, became a maid of honour either to Katherine of Aragon or Anne Boleyn. William had left in 1525 to join Henry Fitzroy's household. But it is the eldest daughter Catherine that history has marked for special mention. For it was she who became the Sixth wife of Henry VIII.

Henry was her third husband. At 17 years of age, in 1529, she had left the Rye House to marry Edward Burrough, who died in 1533. In 1534 she married John Neville, who died in 1543. In 1543 she married Henry VIII and was Queen until 1547, when Henry died. On his death she was given the title 'Dowager Queen', which shows how high Henry had held her in his affections. Indeed, Catherine had conducted herself with great efficiency and aplomb when from July to September in 1544 the King went on his last campaign to France, leaving her as his Regent. There had been a serious 'rift in the lute', as it were, during their short marriage when in 1546 Catherine's fervour with regard to the Protestant faith had led to discussions with the King. During a time when senior members of the Church were trying to restrict further reforms in the hope of a reconciliation with Rome, it's not surprising that her anti-Protestant opponents got to hear of these conversations and a warrant was issued for her arrest. This could have been very serious for her indeed but before her enemies could act she was able to see the warrant and with presence of mind explain to the King that it had simply been her intention to distract him from the pain in his ulcerated leg. Henry was obviously convinced, although not everyone it seemed had been informed of the King's opinion because, whilst out walking together, an armed guard came to arrest her. Soon after Henry's death she married Thomas Seymour, an earlier admirer, and the brother of Jane Seymour and uncle to Henry VI. Catherine died in 1548 after giving birth to her daughter, Mary Seymour.

Of the two other Parr children, William became the first Marquess of Northampton whilst Anne became the Countess of Pembroke

.

As a footnote to Catherine Parr and her association with the Rye House, it is not impossible that she brought Princess Elizabeth, of whom she was very fond, to visit the house in which she grew up. Indeed, the affection between them was mutual. Although there is certainly no evidence to support the idea of a visit, the possibility is not without some credence. What perhaps is more evidential with regard to Elizabeth is that, in 1555, three years before she was proclaimed Queen, Princess Elizabeth was conducted to the Rye House where she resided for a time. She was accompanied by a Privy Counsellor and a large retinue who, it is thought, were spies for Queen Mary (*European Magazine*, 1805). On leaving the Rye House, she would have moved to Hatfield House where, in 1558, she heard of her succession to the throne. In later years, as Queen Elizabeth, she visited her confidante Lord Burghley at Theobalds eight times during her reign. She would then travel on to stay at Hunsdon, a home of her childhood and now in the possession of her kinsman Carey (Lord Hunsdon) and in all likelihood used the toll road, that being the most direct route.

To return to the ownership of the house: in 1526, Andrew died and left the Manor to his heir George. The Rye House remained in the Ogard family until 1559 when, to meet certain debts, George Ogard sold it to William Frankland, a mercer (cloth worker) from London. It was he who owned the Black Lyon inn in Hoddesdon that, up to 1530, was known as the Starre, in 1826 becoming the Salisbury Arms; and which is now once again the Star (albeit with a difference in spelling). In 1566, he married a widow, Joyce or Jocosa Saxey. He died in 1576, although the year of his death has also been given as 1580. In 1581, Joyce Frankland's 23-year-old son from her first marriage was thrown from an unruly horse and killed. He is buried in Stanstead Abbotts Church where a brass to his memory is in the floor of the south aisle. Her grief was enormous and she began to seek out ways in which to give a meaning and a lasting tribute to the lives of her husband and son. Her son had been a scholar at Cambridge and had then gone on to read law at Gray's Inn. With money at her disposal, she became a generous benefactor to Emmanuel and Caius colleges, there creating scholarships and fellowships. In 1587, specifically in memory of her son, she established the Newport Free Grammar School in Essex - now known as the Joyce Frankland Academy, Newport. She died the same year and was buried in the Church of St Leonard in the City of London where a monument was also erected to her memory. Unfortunately, the church was destroyed in the Great Fire of 1666.

In 1598, the Rye House was tenanted by a Mr Anthony Whitfield of London who was chastised for not maintaining the bridge and allowing it to fall into disrepair – so much so in fact that, according to one report, it was impassable.

In 1604, work began to cut a channel from Chadwell Springs, in Hertfordshire, as part of the New River. The spring water carried by the channel, with additional supplies from Amwell Springs and the River Lea, would provide the inhabitants of London with uncontaminated drinking water. Its course was from New Gauge in Hertford to Clerkenwell, Islington and, as it neared the Rye House, it ran parallel with and was a short distance from the right bank of the River Lea. The New River opened in 1613.

The Rye House passed from William Frankland to his son William: "for life with reversion to Hugh Frankland his nephew, for life, and then to the issue male of William. In 1606 Hugh Frankland conveyed his interest in the Manor to William Frankland his nephew, William Frankland the elder having died without issue. In 1619 William Frankland and Lucy his wife sold it to Sir Edward Baesh" (*Victoria History of the Counties of England*, 1912) of Stanstead Bury. Who, according to the eighteenth-century county historian, Sir Henry Chauncy, was a "good and pious man." It is not hard to understand how Chauncy reached this conclusion for it was Baesh who founded the free grammar school in Stanstead Abbotts (the Clock House of today) and who left money to support a school master. He also left money for poor children to be apprenticed to some useful occupation, a cottage for a clerk and a house with land for the vicar. Additionally in 1635, quite some time before his death, he built the alms houses at the foot of Cats Hill to accommodate six poor widows. In 1614, he was a member of parliament for Grantham and again for Stamford in 1628. During the Civil War he was a neutral and maintained his neutrality throughout the conflict.

Sir Edward Baesh died in 1653. He had remained childless despite two marriages and so the Rye House estate was entailed on a cousin, Ralph Baesh, from the other side of the family. He was knighted after the Restoration in recognition of his financial support to the royal cause during the Civil War. In the last year of his life, 1676, Edmund Feilde bought Stanstead Bury and its estate. This included the Rye House, which would remain in the possession of his descendants for a number of years.

In 1683, at the time of the Plot, the House, although owned by the Feildes, was tenanted by Richard Rumbold – who according to

Nathaniel Salmon (writing in 1728) "threatened Sir Thomas Feild his landlord with words highly impudent, and Countenance that had fire and sword in it." (The part played by the Rye House and indeed Richard Rumbold in the plot to assassinate King Charles II is covered in the next chapter, 'The Rye House Plot'.)

It was during this period (mid-to-late seventeenth century) that the Malting was established. As to the fate of Fallowes Row – or Flowings Roe, Slowings Row or even the corne chambers and stables, to use its alternative names – there are drawings that show it in place up to 1784 but none thereafter.

The demolition of the House took place at the end of the seventeenth century (Smith, 1993). Writing in the early 1720s, Nathaniel Salmon (1728) noted that: "There is yet a part of the old building standing at least something built in the old Form when the house first decayed." By the end of the seventeenth century, the House would have been over 200 years old and no doubt showing signs of age; and indeed, it had been remarked that in Rumbold's time the House was in a dilapidated state. Conversely, with its thick walls, the Gatehouse was more robust and consequently more able to withstand the rigours of time; moreover, the cost of demolishing such a solid building may also have been a factor. The House, apart from the Gatehouse, was rebuilt at the end of the seventeenth century (Smith, 1993) but the materials used in its construction are unknown. Charnock's drawing from 1780 quite clearly shows the

Charnock's image with the obvious brickwork of the Gatehouse. Neither his depiction of the Maltings nor the row of vegetation (see below) are clearly shown in this photograph.

J.M.W. Turner, Gatehouse at
Rye House, Hertfordshire,
c.1793–4

Gatehouse in its brick-built splendour but the rebuild's appearance
has the look of an external render, whereas a watercolour by
Turner from 1793 of the Gatehouse and the rebuild shows the
latter clad in weatherboard. (A colour print of Turner's watercolour
is on display in the Gatehouse.) A later drawing by Ellis from 1806
does give the rebuild a different colouring to that of the Gatehouse
but whether or not it is weatherboard is unclear; while a drawing
by Edridge published 1824 gives the rebuild a further 'external
render look' with the only sign of weatherboard shown in the gable
on the northern side of the House. Conversely, Buckler's illustration
of 1833, in particular, gives the rebuild a similar hue and
representation to that of the Gatehouse with both looking to have
been built as one! What is known is that the rebuild was an L-
shaped two-storeys-with-attic building with mullion-and-transom
windows. It is further known that it was added to the north wall of
the Gatehouse with its east side wall set inside the remains of the
Curtain wall. As to when the rebuild was demolished, there are
illustrations up to 1833 which show the Gatehouse and rebuild,
whilst a Tithe Map from 1840 again shows the rebuild in place.
(There is more with regard to the rebuild, when it was demolished
and perhaps the significance of the year 1840 below.)

Buckler's 1833 illustration.
(Gilmore Hankey Kirke Ltd)

The curtain wall with the
remnants of a brick barrelled
vault. (Photo by the author)

The Rye House, Hertfordshire, with Fallowes Row to the foreground. (Copper engraved print published in Francis Grose's *Antiquities of England and Wales*, 1786)

From the late eighteenth century, the Gatehouse was used as the workhouse for the poor of Stanstead Abbotts. It has been suggested that the Maltings was similarly used as indeed was the rebuilt Rye House. Grose (1783), however, wrote that "[t]he gate [Gatehouse] is now used as a workhouse to the Parish of Stanstead Abbots" but made no mention of any other building being used for the same purpose. Remarkably, a few years earlier, in 1777, there were 50 inmates, who in the main would have been made up of the old, the sick, the infirm and children. Even allowing for the harsh conditions, it does seem rather implausible that the relatively small Gatehouse rooms might fit the necessary 50 beds and, presumably, an area for meals, especially given the requirement to separate the sexes. Moreover, often an area was needed to educate the children and to hold religious services. The able bodied received outdoor relief, either cash or in kind (bread or other goods), or a combination of the two; this allowed them to receive alms yet live in their homes. In 1834, with the introduction of the New Poor Law, outdoor relief was prohibited and the only assistance available was to be found inside the workhouse. Admittedly, workhouse conditions were made so abhorrent that only the desperate would enter but nevertheless there were those who still needed to be accommodated. Previous accounts of the period would suggest that all of the poor of Stanstead Abbotts, as well as those from neighbouring parishes, were moved to the workhouse in Ware in 1834, even though the new Union workhouse wasn't completed until 1839-40! Harper (1904), however, was of the opinion that the Gatehouse was used as a workhouse until 1840; while from the *Penny Magazine* dated 16th May 1840 comes the following, which is very enlightening: "The only portion of the Rye-House now standing is an embattled gate-house, built of brick and ornamented with a handsome stone Gothic doorway. This was formerly used as a workhouse and is still inhabited by some of the old women who occupied it before the Poor Law Amendment Act (1834) rendered it necessary to provide other accommodation for the paupers of the Union which the Parish of Stanstead Abbotts is included." Curiously, there is a very similar, indeed almost plagiaristic, passage in Andrews (1902) in which the author instead considers that the "old women" still inhabited the workhouse "until about 1805".

It is well documented that initially the Ware Guardians continued to use local parish workhouses and that the Poor Law Commissioners in 1836 authorised £1,000 for the upgrade of said local parish workhouses. It is hard to determine whether or not

Rye House workhouse received an upgrade but what is known from the Overseers Accounts from the Parish of Stanstead Abbots is that, on the 11th March 1839, the removal of "Elizabeth Sibley & her two children to the Ware Union for provision" is only overshadowed by the removal of "Deadman from the Rye to… near Albury he having a fractured limb." In 1842 two names are listed as receiving a pension: Hughes £1.19.0 and Johnson £2.11.6; while the last entry was on 20th October 1845 listing Hughes £1.19.0. It would appear that although the building was no longer classified as a workhouse and despite the New Poor Law, some occupants had remained, as the article from the *Penny Magazine* suggested, and received a pension up to or perhaps after they were removed or no longer in need.

It is claimed that by the early part of the nineteenth century, the Manor of Rye House descended to a Miss Fielde who sold it soon after marrying a Captain Upton. (The variable spelling of the surname Feilde, Fielde or even Feild is no less remarkable than the variable spelling of the surname Baeshe, Baesh, Bashe or even Barsh.) Further claims abound; the following testimonies, although in some cases flawed, will nevertheless help us to unravel some of the truth.

The 1839 Tithe Awards for plot 577, which was Rye Farm and part of the Rye House Estate, lists the Fielde family as the registered owners, with a William Webb as the occupier and a Miss Isabelle Sophia Georgiana Fielde also listed as an owner as well as an Infant and Tenant in Tail. The *Penny Magazine* from 1840 states that the Rye House at that time was owned by the Fielde family; while the *Gentleman's Magazine* spells the previously mentioned Miss Fielde's full name as Miss Isabella Georgina Feilde, only child of the late William Henry Feilde Esq., of Netherfield House, Herts, and states that she married a Lewis Upton Esq., of Glyde Court, Co Louth, late 9th Lancers, in October 1844. Another source yet again spells her name differently – Isabella Sophia Georgiana Feilde – and further gives September as the month of marriage, although the year remains the same. Finally, Whitley and Andrews (1888) state that Lewis Upton, who married Miss Feilde, sold the Rye House along with the celebrated tavern to the late Mr Teale in May 1867. This last entry is at odds with the Auction of the Rye House estate in 1867 (see below), which included the Rye House and indeed the 'celebrated tavern'; but nevertheless an element of truth would still discredit the claim that the Manor of Rye House was sold soon after Miss Feilde married and, in particular, that it was sold to Charles Booth (of Booth's Gin). Booth did at about this time purchase the Netherfield estate that included Netherfield House, the former home of William Henry Feilde, so perhaps the misconception stemmed from this. Moreover, in 1867, Booth further purchased the Warren, Rye Farm, some land east of it and more, and was subsequently responsible for improving the toll road across the meadows. It is further claimed that Anthony Upton, a wine merchant in partnership with Henry Rumbold, purchased the Rye House from Paul Feilde who had owned it for many years. This is all the more confusing first because it comes from Andrews (1902), the co-author of the above publication from 1888, and because it is believed that in 1783 on the death of Paul Feilde, who died without issue, the Rye House Estate passed to a cousin, the Rector of Eastwick, Thomas Feilde. It then passed to his son William Henry Feilde, then to William Henry Feilde Jr and finally to Miss Feilde.

The involvement of Anthony Upton continues to bewilder because he is again credited by another writer as having bought the property, only much earlier (c.1680), while in partnership, this time, with Richard Rumbold. With what has been previously written, this would seem unlikely; and Salmon's (1728) account of Rumbold's argument with 'Thomas Field' his landlord in 1683 only emphasises the point further. Nevertheless, with Upton's name seemingly linked with the Rye House, a feasible explanation must surely be available. It has been suggested that perhaps Upton had acted as a guarantor to Rumbold's widow and became the tenant as an act of charity (Stanstead Abbots Local History Society, 2017). It has also been claimed that Richard Rumbold had forged a connection with the Uptons by marrying Anthony Upton's sister. Rumbold married the widow of a maltster, but there are no recorded marriages in Hertfordshire for a female with the surname Upton as far back as 1600. On the 28th October 1672, a Sus Haley married Robert Dockerill; on the 12th April 1676, a Sus Haley married Richard Rumbold. If this is the same person, and it would seem very likely, it's interesting that the surname 'Haley' is listed instead of 'Dockerill', which suggests that Haley was her maiden name; although the possibility exists (dependent upon her age) that she married as an Upton and became widowed outside of Hertfordshire prior to 1672. On the 30th September 1707, Sus Rumbold (although here her last married name is listed) further married a George Raymond. Armitage (1948) writes that the Rumbold family and the Upton family were later united by marriage. And indeed there was a marriage between a John Upton, a relative of Anthony Upton, and a Mary Murton on the 29th December 1703. Which is all very uncertain; but what is certain is that an Upton, through marriage, did have a connection with the Rye House, the former residence of Richard Rumbold.

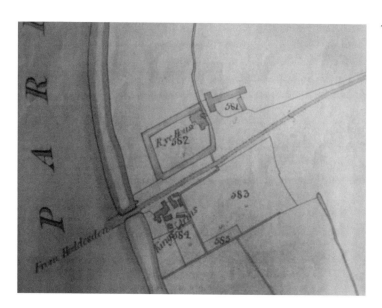

The Tithe Map from 1840.

The 1840 Tithe Map shows a different shape to the Maltings to that of the original. It now resembles the shape of the letter T due to an additional build added at its west end. One of the projections to the south has gone, whilst the north projection at the east end of the original build has also been (PIC) removed.

In the mid-1840s, Mr William Henry Teale leased the Rye House and 50 acres of land with the purpose of making it an attraction in the form of a pleasure garden to those in search of an 'outing'. Soon after, he also obtained the licence for the public house that, according to some, dates from 1600 and, to others, from 1756 and changed its name from the King's Arms. What the name changed to is unclear, however. One account has it as the Rye House Hotel from the outset whilst another has it as the Rye House Inn, not becoming the Rye House Hotel until 1904. Then in a newspaper article from 1850 it is called Ye Old Rye House Inn while an American traveller writing in 1857 names it the Rye House Tavern. If that weren't confusing enough, an advertisement naming W.H. Teale as the proprietor and dated in between 1867 and 1876 has it as the Old Rye House Inn and Fishery. An undated drawing names it Ye Olde Rye House while a Plan of Auction map from 1881 (see below) has it as Ye Rye House with an Ordnance Survey map from 1895–6 then naming it the Rye House Hotel. A postcard from 1914 has it once again as Ye Olde Rye House Inn while further early-twentieth-century postcards and photographs name it either Ye Rye House Hotel or again as Ye Rye House. Further Ordnance Survey maps dated 1915 and 1939 continue to name it as the Rye House Hotel, while in between 1969–71 it was Ye Olde Rye House Hotel. The confusion is almost complete. In 1988 it was known as Rye's and from an undated newspaper article from the twentieth century we have this:"The pub is once again known as the King's Arms, and its sign shows Charles II who nearly lost his life in the 1683 plot."Today, it is known as The Rye House – I think!

The area was already made popular with anglers by Izaak Walton's book *The Compleat Angler*, published in 1653. Later, in 1845 Mr Thomas Watson, landlord of the King's Arms, contributed to this popularity by applying to the owners of the newly opened railway line to Hertford (1843) for the train to stop here for anglers. With no station, travellers requested to be let off or waved a red flag to board. By 1846, Rye House had become a station but it wasn't until 1849 that it obtained a platform and a booking office. The platform incidentally had to be extended at least on two occasions as the destination grew in popularity. With the development of the railways, access to areas within a short distance from home became possible and, with the new train link, Rye House would become a very popular destination with Londoners in particular.

That said, it would seem that the Gatehouse and the Maltings as attractions had a slow preamble to future success because around 1853 there was no formal bridge across the moat: instead, the visitor was required to negotiate a 'rotting tree trunk'!

By 1856, the north, south and west arms of the moat were being used to grow watercress. This was an important Hertfordshire industry on account of the chalk streams in the county and the good travel links to the London markets. At the Rye House, watercress continued to be grown until during the Second World War, when the water table dropped dramatically.

A guide book published in the same year informs the reader that the Castle Hall (formerly known as the Maltings) had been restored and was now capable of accommodating 1,000 people. Indeed, the roof had been partially thatched and tiled, a large bay window had been installed at the eastern end of the building while the interior contained rows of tables and chairs ready for the influx of visitors. The book also describes the interior of the Hall with its "old carved chimney piece, its Elizabethan panel and wainscoting – the iron dogs where the 'yule log was wont to blaze', the rude construction of the building – girders of roughly hewn trees with portions of bark still adhering to them."The Hall as well as the first-floor room contained the paintings, tapestries, armour and antiquities that were on display. The first-floor room had amongst its exhibits a canopied bedstead, with Florentine silk damask hangings, that was presented as having once belonged to Queen Elizabeth I and removed from her hunting lodge at Epping Forest. This was positioned in the south-west corner and met the eye when entering the room from the spiral staircase. The guide book also mentions that a conservatory was in place adjoining the west wall and that interestingly the entrance to the subterranean passage was full of water. Equally interesting was the discovery in 1852 of 13 antique vases, most of which were intact, and a silver coin dating from the reign of Henry I discovered when the foundations of the enclosure wall were excavated. The grounds are remarked upon as being ornamented with a hermitage, a shell grotto, statuary, floral arbours and rustic temples on the banks of the River; while the grass area within the Moated Enclosure took on the guise of a garden with benches here and there for visitors. The list of activities was also quite extensive and included rowing, sailing, cricket, trap ball, archery, quoits and a bowling green, while three miles of preserved angling was available to those who preferred a more sedate pastime.

A drawing from 1858 by an unknown artist shows an extension to the north of the Gatehouse. This addition, it is claimed, was probably built in 1857 (Smith, 1993) although in an engraving published by Rock & Co., London, probably from the 1840s, the extension

Rock & Co; The Rye House, Broxbourne; Herts (The Image Collection, Hertfordshire Archives and Local Studies)

Rye House. Broxbourne. Herts.

appears to be included. The number of battlements and the amount of brickwork is too extensive for it to be the Curtain Wall alone and the join with the extension can actually be seen. The numbers 1, 8, 2 and 8 can be seen in the bottom left corner of the image which have been construed to be the year 1828, although preceding the numbers is a numero sign, which perhaps instead indicates a reference number. Moreover, the clothing of both the men and the women look to be from a later era than the 1820s. The women's bell-shaped skirts are matched with coal-scuttle bonnets and capes in the style of the mid-nineteenth century; while the silk top hat and flared frock-coat of a male figure, inspired by Prince Albert, is again mid-nineteenth century, being particularly characteristic of the 1840s. However, the image also shows a crossing of some sort with handrails to the front of the Gatehouse; but do they flank a proper bridge or the tree trunk, later to become the 'rotting tree trunk' of 1853? If it's not the tree trunk, is the image instead from a later date, perhaps nearer to 1857? Probably not. An unpublished drawing by James Bourne from 1845 shows the rear of the Gatehouse as having far more battlements than the original structure, which either denotes artistic licence or the presence of the extension in the 1840s.

The building measured approximately 18 feet (540cm) north to south and 17 feet (510cm) west to east and was in fact a suite of private apartments with its own staircase. In effect, it was the third Rye House. It is assumed that at one time it was used as an employee's residence because a Record of Duties on Land Values dated 1910 for the Pleasure Gardens at Rye House lists Christie & Co. as owners and W. Abel as occupier. Later in its history it became part of the museum and the ground floor came to be called the parlour, while the first-floor room with the now-added Queen Elizabeth I bed came to be known as Queen Elizabeth's Bedroom. Complete flummery, of course, as she certainly couldn't have slept in a Victorian extension but, with the bed supposed to have come from her hunting lodge, it added an historic element. However, an extract from the *European Magazine* dated January 1805, much before the era of the Pleasure Gardens, could possibly throw additional light on Queen Elizabeth's past association with the Rye House and with the Gatehouse in particular. With reference to the Gatehouse, the extract reads: "Tradition states, that till within a few years, the chamber of the Princess (which was called Queen Elizabeth's chamber) was to be seen and that part of the ancient furniture and some inscriptions, upon the walls remained." With only one room suitable enough to accommodate a princess, it is assumed the author is referring to the first-floor room. The Bedroom in the Victorian extension also had a window in the north wall and

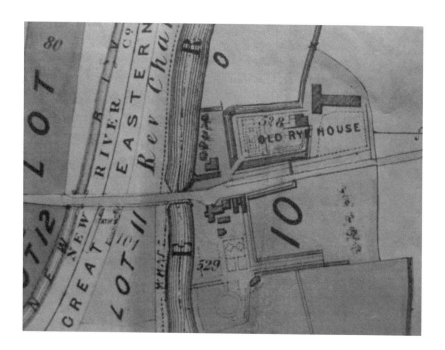

another in the west wall. The top of the building was crenelated, while the remains of the original fifteenth-century curtain wall were included, but not bonded, to become part of the building's east wall.

The Auction Plan 1867.

In the 1867 Plan of the Rye House Estate for Sale by Auction, as expected, the extension rather than the rebuilt Rye House is shown, which suggests that the year of the latter's demolition lay between 1840 and 1867. Interestingly, because the Tithe Map shows the rebuild, a magazine article from 1840 could either pinpoint that year as the year of the House's demolition or be completely misleading. The article, as previously mentioned, describes the embattled Gatehouse as "[t]he only portion of the Rye House now standing." The article also included a drawing of the Gatehouse with the rebuild that showed no sign of the moat while the turret still had its arcade with ruinous brickwork above, which were details from an earlier period. And indeed, the earlier drawings and engravings aside, the drawing illustrated in the *Bon Bouche* magazine in 1823 and supposedly 'taken on the spot' shows the turret as depicted in the Ellis drawing from 1806. So although the drawing featured in the *Penny Magazine* is from an earlier period, the possibility that the author considered the rebuilt Rye House to be inferior to the original House and so didn't consider it necessary to include it in his description cannot be overlooked! However, if in 1840 there were no other buildings than the Gatehouse present then this is an important piece of testimony.

The Plan also gives every indication that the north-eastern section of the moat, from just south of the Gatehouse to where it bends to join the northern arm, had been completely filled in. From what's known of the early history of the Rye House, it's believed that the moat had undergone a reduction in its width since its construction. Consequently, early drawings and engravings from 1777 onwards, like the example taken from the *Lady's Magazine*, 1795, show a foreground to the Gatehouse where once there would have been open water. There is a very clear image from the Oldfield Collection (with an unprecise date in between 1700 and 1800) that depicts water on both sides of an entrance path that runs level with the water itself! The remaining images are either difficult to decipher

Oldfield's image showing the moat either side of a path.

Rye Houfe Hertfordfhire.
Pub. April 21, 1784 by S. Hooper.

or, if a date is given, it is not always reliable. The perspective of Sparrow's drawing (1784), which is the prominent image on the front cover, only allows the moat to the south of the Gatehouse to be included albeit with a visible causeway, while Charnock's (1780) is hard to make sense of. A row of vegetation which could be construed as the bank of the moat is actually shown forward of the Maltings. Whereas Rawles' engraving with the dubious publication date of 1805 (as explained in the chapter 'The Gatehouse and Moated Enclosure') shows a path at a similar level to its surrounds, like that shown in Oldfield's, but gives no clear indication that the moat is present; although two sets of post-and-rail fence in the direction of the moat could possibly be related to the still-present moat. An undated drawing from the *Penny Magazine*, with the turret shown to be in a farther state of deterioration than that depicted in the engraving by Rawles, has people walking and a dog running ahead over the area presumably between the same two sets of post-and-rail fence, while Smith's image (with the equally dubious publication date of 1807) shows a plank of wood spanning the east arm of the moat. Turner's watercolour dated 1793–4 has no obvious crossing to be seen and again it's hard to determine if a

The Gatehouse and the rebuilt Rye House. (S. Sparrow, from *The Antiquities of England & Wales*, by Francis Grose, London: S. Hooper, 1784)

Buckler's 1826 illustration.
(Gilmore Hankey Kirke Ltd)

watercourse to the front of the Gatehouse is represented as the colouring on both sides of the footpath allows for speculation.

The speculation continues even with the drawing from the *Bon Bouche* publication in 1823. Here the moat could be coaxed into existence by comparing the direction and the bend in the path with that of the causeway in J.C. Buckler's illustration from 1826. He shows a fairly wide expanse of water on both sides of the Gatehouse entrance and crossed by a causeway, with an assumed culvert to the foreground. Whereas an undated sketch by A. Bourne (although certainly post 1806) shows no sign of the moat in the north-east arm, has raised ground with a path to the Gatehouse entrance and ducks on the south-east arm. In 1827, a further volume of Clutterbuck's publication, *The History and Antiquities of the County of Hertford*, informs the reader that the Rye House "was formerly entirely surrounded by a moat which has been partly filled in". The wording here is very ambiguous: he could either have been referring to a reduction in the moat's width or instead to a section of the moat that had been filled in. And bearing in mind that 1827 was the date of publication, perhaps when Clutterbuck wrote the section on the Rye House, part of the moat had indeed been filled in. However, the tome also includes an image of the Gatehouse by Edridge, with the assumed correct date of 1824, which shows the north-east arm of the moat well and truly open. Two years later and

Buckler's illustration and thereafter a further illustration from 1832 show a moat either side of the causeway, while the Tithe Map from 1840 also shows a complete east arm. In short, it's possible that part of the east arm of the moat had been filled in but inconsistent and unclear images and a lack of detail from earlier historians makes it difficult to be assured of this. From 1840 onwards, and certainly by 1853 when the 'rotting tree trunk' came into its own, the presumption is that unless the moat was filled in and then dug out, it remained for a number of years in an open condition.

With Buckler in particular considered to be accurate (Smith, 1975), it is hoped that the Plan from 1867 is equally so; but given that watercress was being grown on a commercial basis in the north, south and west arms of the moat and with the plant best grown in abundant and fresh clear water, it would seem most unlikely that this section of the moat, as depicted on the Plan, was completely filled in. Thereafter, Ordnance Survey maps from 1880 and 1896 show part of the northern arm of the moat as being much reduced in width; while again the area to the front of the Gatehouse looks to be devoid of water. Hopefully, Winstone (1889) can be relied upon in this instance to offer an insight when he writes:"The moat, formerly surrounding the manor, house and garden, now also surrounds the garden and buildings. It is, however, narrowed to a ditch in front of the gatehouse; and a little bridge spans it". The ditch to which he alludes is a far cry from the expanse of yesteryear,

Buckler's 1832 illustration.
(Gilmore Hankey Kirke Ltd)

The interior of the Retainer's Hall. (Gilmore Hankey Kirke Ltd)

but at least the water was flowing. Photographs from the period 1907 to 1910 show the area to the front of the Gatehouse with varied amounts of vegetation to the right and left of the entrance but with always a defined causeway or path. An Ordnance Survey map from 1915, however, again shows no sign of water in the north-eastern arm but the 1925 guide book assures us "that the moat still flows under the path". Beyond this date, what remained of the moat was becoming choked with vegetation and indeed a photograph of the front of the Gatehouse from 1930 and the Ordnance Survey map from 1939 show a building attached to the Gatehouse at an angle from the Curtain Wall to the Retainers' Hall.

With the on-going development of the Pleasure Gardens and with the subsequent reduction in the width of the moat, it was no longer necessary for visitors who approached the Gatehouse to cross an expanse of water. As a consequence, it would undoubtedly have prevented those imbibed with the beverage of their choice available from the tavern built in the forecourt of the Retainers' Hall (formerly known as the Castle Hall) from entering the moat in an undignified manner. Instead, and certainly for a period anyway, they were able to enter a ditch in an undignified manner and, once having extracted themselves, were at liberty to pay a visit to the wash-and-brush-up facility, also known as the 'poo, piddle and plunge' by the Curtain Wall/extension.

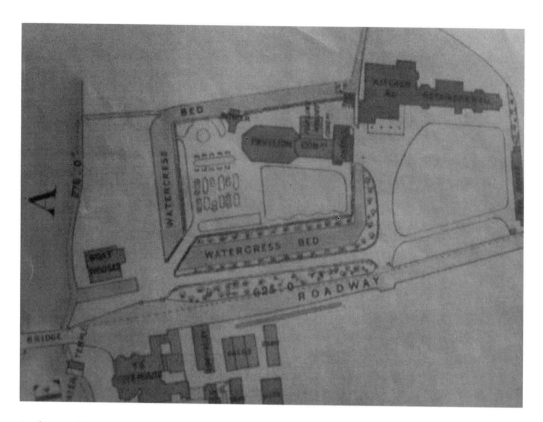

At the south-west corner of the moat, the 1881 Auction Plan (see photo) shows a causeway or a bridge – a footbridge is indicated on later Ordnance Survey maps – before the entrance to the gardens. A causeway is in place to this day with culverts, while the two chimney shafts used as gateposts also remain (see the chapter 'The Gatehouse and Moated Enclosure'). The Plan also shows the gardens within the moated enclosure and a boathouse at the Quay approximately next to where the slipway is today, which itself was a water-filled cutting.

Sometime in between 1864 and 1870 the Great Bed of Ware was bought as an attraction. It was put on display and a fee was charged (see the chapter 'The Great Bed of Ware').

By 1865, Rye House Station was regarded as the busiest excursion route on the whole of the Great Eastern Railway out from London. Indeed, during Whitsun of that year 15,000 people visited the Rye House by train alone, a further 7,000 by horse-drawn carriage, whilst between 1875 and 1914 tens of thousands, mainly East

The Auction Plan, 1881.

The Great Bed of Ware, 1590–1600 (V&A Museum no. W.47:1 to 28-1931. Techniques: Oak, carved and originally painted, with panels of marquetry. Artist/designer: Marquetry by Hans Vredeman de Vries (1527–1604). Place: Ware, England.)

Enders, flocked to Rye House packed like sardines into the train carriages.

In 1867, the Rye House Estate was broken up for auction, although the 1881 Auction Plan gives the previous purchase date of Lot 10 as 14th July 1868. This lot consisted of the Gatehouse and Moated Enclosure, the land west to the River Lea, north-east and east to the first ditch and south to the Great Eastern Railway London-to-Cambridge Line, all of which encompassed and included the public house. The land north of the moat known as 'Old Rye Mead' in between the Lea and the feeder stream was included in Lot 1.

In 1870 the cast-iron window frames fronting the public house were installed. They came from a house in Cheshunt.

In 1876, Mr W.H. Teale died and the estate was run by members of the family. Although on the 20th March 1877, "[b]y direction of the Executors and Devisees of the late Mr W.H. Teale, the Freeholder, deceased", the public house and the pleasure and recreation grounds with the other "mediaeval attractions" were to be auctioned. The lease was for 30 years and included 24 acres of land. An article in the *Hertfordshire Mercury* dated 24th March 1877 reads as follows: "The business at the Rye House will it is announced be carried on by the family of the late Mr Teale as usual. The customary festivities will take place on Easter Monday when there will be fireworks, military and quadrille bands and dancing".

The Retainer's Hall in the 1920s. (Taken from the guide book, 1925)

By 1880, a new room adjoined the Retainers' Hall on the Stanstead side; the Conservatory at the west end of the Gatehouse now had forcing houses to the north of it; while a new Dining Hall near the Maze had had cathedral glass windows installed allowing for expansive views of the surrounding countryside. Additional attractions and improvements included a bowling alley, bower, maze, the Great Bed of Ware, tea rooms and a large kitchen at the west end of the Retainers' Hall to cater for the many diners. Three years later, the interior of the Retainers' Hall had been renovated and the gardens remodelled by Mrs Teale. In addition, a drawing from an earlier year shows the 'Grand Staircase' which still led to 'Ye Four Gabled Refectory'. This was an old-fashioned tea room kept strictly for mothers meetings and temperance gatherings.

In 1881, a nearby boating accident claimed the lives of two visitors. Father and son were heading upstream with two others in a small boat when it capsized and they drowned. It was also the year that the freehold again came up for sale. Messrs Cronin were instructed by the executors of the late W.H. Teale Esq. to sell the exceedingly valuable estate known as the Rye House by auction on the 6th July 1881. The lease was now for 27 years although the acreage still amounted to 24. Then from the *Herts Guardian* dated 21st June 1881 this: "The Rye House. Messrs Cronin advertise the Freehold of this noted Hotel… It is requisite to state that the forthcoming sale of the Freehold does not affect the business of the Hotel or the lesseeship of the present proprietors who are booking largely for the present season, and an extensive business is anticipated." The following year, however, an article from a local paper dated Saturday 12th August 1882 names Messrs Teale & Co as the proprietors of "this favourite place" when reporting on the immense numbers that visited the Pleasure Gardens the previous week-end.

But although the numbers were great, the success of the enterprise was not appreciated by all. In particular, some local residents were more than a little alarmed at the disorderly conduct on display from a good many of the visitors who included amongst their number some intoxicated children who, not to be outdone, contributed to the foul language on offer. People had left behind their claustrophobic conurbations for a few hours and were intent upon having a good time within a country setting; and their sheer numbers were bound to encourage some rowdiness. Benjamin Moran, an American who visited the Rye House as early as 1857, remarked that it was a "resort of too many vulgar Londoners to be desirable" while Senior (1877) wrote that "a large number of fairly dressed men… and women of the same class overseen in drink before two o'clock in the day I had never seen before and would fain hope shall never see again." Indeed the boisterous behaviour was not confined to the immediate area as those arriving by horse-drawn charabanc often had their arrival heralded by a trumpet or horn, blown by the driver's mate as the coach passed through Hoddesdon.

A fracas at the Pleasure Garden that was spoken of in the House of Commons is also worthy of note. In 1885, Catholic excursionists from Deptford and Orangemen clashed. It was first thought that swords were drawn by the Orangemen and amongst those set upon was one Reverend M.P. Fannun who was superintending the excursionists. A report from the Chief Constable of the County, however, dismissed any claim that swords were drawn as none were seen by the police. Sheathed swords, sticks, umbrellas, quart pots and bottles, yes; but drawn swords, definitely not! Rowdiness amongst some continued well into the 1920s when often PC Oliver and his horse 'Benny Ally' were called upon to clear the area of drunken visitors.

By 1898, new attractions and additions were to be found, amongst which was the New Jubilee Pavilion that measured 120 feet long by 50 feet wide, had cathedral glass windows and could seat 500 people to dine at any one time. Further delights included a fancy bazaar, pony and donkey rides, an American bowling alley and a steam merry-go-round. The *Hackney Express and Shoreditch Observer* wrote in the same year: "attractions increase each year everything associated with Rye House has improved." In 1904 the estate was acquired by Messrs Christie & Co. the Hoddesdon brewers with Mr William Abel as manager. The First World War undoubtedly affected visitor numbers as young men and women disappeared in one way or another doing their 'bit' for king and country. After the war, the estate recovered and under the guidance of Mr A.J. Vince continued to obtain good visitor numbers into the 1920s. For example, 20,000 people were estimated to have frequented the public house alone during the Whitsun Holiday of 1921. In addition, the official programme of a grand fete and pageant held at the Pleasure Gardens in 1924 stated that as many as 100,000 persons visited annually. The proceedings were opened by HRH Princess Arthur of Connaught. Indeed, Royal patronage was no stranger to the Gatehouse and surrounding Pleasure Gardens as His Highness the Nawab Nazin of Bengal visited several times during 1872–3 to take advantage of the fishing etcetera. Nevertheless, by the end of the 1920s the days of large visitor numbers were over. The advent of the motor car and a change in people's recreational pursuits sounded the death toll for the Pleasure Gardens.

RYE HOUSE-THE GARDENS.

The guide book from 1925 shows that the arrival of the motor car had been catered for: the Boat House was now a garage with the area adjacent to it set aside as a parking area. The guide book also catalogues 190 antiquities, artefacts and paintings on display. The list is far too extensive to be included in full but here is a selection of the most interesting items:

The gardens. (Gilmore Hankey Kirke Ltd)

1　A painting of the Battle on the Bridge between Herts and Essex during the Civil War (This it is assumed was the battle which occurred in Hemsted on a bridge over the River Gade in 1650.)

2　Water Colour picture of Rye House (This watercolour was by Turner, a print of which is now in the gateway.)

3　Pair of prints of Rye House and Nether Hall

4　Water Colour picture of Nether Hall

5　Box of human bones found in the subterranean apartment

6　Type of crossbow used in warfare from about 1370 to 1490

7　A copy of the first letter from the Duke of Monmouth in connection with the Rye House Plot to Charles II, 1683

8　Plan of the Rye House as used at the State Trial in 1683

9　Painting of Richard Rumbold

10　Painting of the Hall of Cheshunt Great House

11　Coloured picture of the Great Bed of Ware

12　A portion of the first Atlantic Cable laid by the *Great Eastern* in 1865

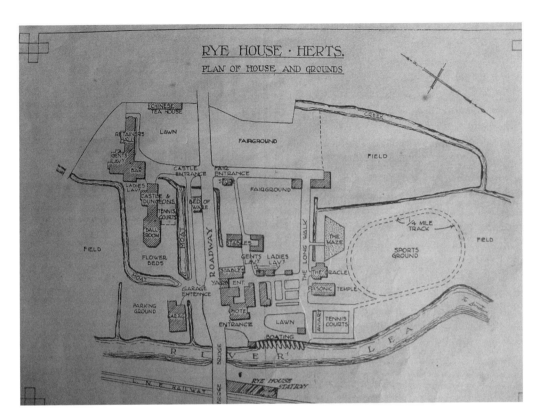

RYE HOUSE · HERTS.
PLAN OF HOUSE AND GROUNDS

Map of the house and grounds from the 1925 guide book.

13 A carved-oak Jacobean dower chest

14 Queen Elizabeth's Bedstead, sixteenth-century Florentine

15 Pair of sixteenth- and seventeenth-century keys

16 Bell-mouth musket, seventeenth century

17 Facsimile of the Warrant for the Execution of Charles I, 29th January 1649

18 Print of Henry Jenkins who died at the great age of 169

19 Painting of the Procession of Jonas and Nellie Nettleby, claimants of the Dunmow Flitch, 20th June 1751

20 The Conspirators' Table richly carved

21 A matchlock, about 1600

22 An Elizabethan halberd

23 Seventeenth-century stone crossbow

24 A painting of James Warman, the Hermit of Hertford Heath

25 A double-barrel flint-lock musket, about 1700

26 A very rare goat-foot lever, used for stringing crossbows of the fourteenth and fifteenth centuries.

In 1928, Christie's Brewery was acquired by the Cannon Brewery. The purchase not only included the public house and grounds but also the Gatehouse and the Retainers' Hall. It was during this time that several of the paintings were removed.

In 1930, Cannon was acquired by Taylor Walker & Co. and again the Gatehouse and Retainers' Hall were included in the sale. By this time, the visitor numbers had declined dramatically and the estate began to fall into disrepair. Even so, for 3d you could enter the Gatehouse and there be met by a rustic guide (see the chapter 'The Gatehouse and Moated Enclosure'). Watercress was for sale at 3d a bunch and tied with a strip of willow whilst a fair continued to be held in the grounds on bank holidays.

A photograph from the early 1930s shows the Retainers' Hall with tables and chairs in readiness for customers, while a visitor to the Gatehouse remarks that "a fair was held in and around the grounds on bank holidays". In 1935, however, the Gatehouse had a fire, which in all probability was the result of arson. A photograph of the first-floor room taken soon afterwards shows various items of furniture and armoury still intact but with part of the tapestry on the north wall hanging in tatters: the floor to the north of the building is still very much in evidence, if strewn with debris from the fire; there is no roof and the windows are unglazed. From then on, the Gatehouse was neglected and no longer used as an attraction or museum. A photograph from the late 1930s shows the lower front and the south wall of the Gatehouse almost hidden by unkempt vegetation.

In 1934–5, an area to the south of the public house became a speedway track. Prior to this, the area was used as a sports ground in the Pleasure Garden complex and then as a horse-racing trotting track. Incidentally, the modern go-kart track was built on the old speedway track.

From 1935 onwards and during the war years, the Pavilion, which had been transformed in the early part of the twentieth century into the Palais de Danse ballroom, although looking shabby and in a state of disrepair, was still used as a dancing venue as well as for roller skating. The boating facilities were also popular at this time, in particular with North Americans stationed in Hunsdon. Indeed, at that time Mr Sykes ran the boating operation and employed small boys to retrieve boats abandoned by the rowers who had made their way back to Hunsdon or elsewhere.

Armitage (1948) describes how, when visiting the Gatehouse, he was shocked and appalled by the spectacle that greeted him. First a crudely painted sign expounding the delights of roller skating caught his attention with the additional information that it cost 6d to watch. The ballroom was not well received either, being even shabbier by this time and vilified in the same vein as an eyesore of a shed now obscuring the entrance to the Gatehouse, which he considered to be vandalism of the worst kind. The once pristine and immaculate gardens were overgrown with brambles and matted with weeds, while headless statues and other debris, some of it from the Gatehouse, were deposited at random. He also mentions a fair that, although expressing no animosity towards it, he nevertheless considered to be out of place in such an historic setting. Also in 1948, a drawing by Hanslip Fletcher for the *Sunday Times* shows a ramshackle Retainers' Hall with the Gatehouse very much in need of attention. In 1951, the Department of the Environment makes no mention of the Retainers' Hall, which suggests that the building had been demolished by this date.

The Gatehouse continued to deteriorate into the 1950s: there was no roof and the vegetation was threatening to overpower the building. But although with the adjoining conservatory and ballroom it was in urgent need of attention, it wasn't in a dangerous condition as the above usage and an article from the *Times* dated May 1951 can testify to: "and though elder bushes are growing in the depth of humus on the roofless upper floor their roots have not penetrated the floor boards." Encouragingly, on the 4th December 1951, it was listed as an Ancient Monument by the Ministry of Works and, with the aid of a preservation fund instigated by the East Herts Archaeological Society with an initial £100 donation, work began as advised by the Ministry of Works. Trees and bushes were cleared from the front, and debris removed from the upper floor, the newel stair and from the interior. The ivy that covered the south side of the battlements was removed without any damage to the brickwork, which was revealed to be in good condition. The moat was not attempted.

Once all this had been achieved, attention was turned to the fabric of the building. A temporary roof was suggested and estimates were sought. This work along with other projects ran into thousands of pounds and so, with £75 left in the kitty, assistance was looked for elsewhere. The brewery owners felt unable to spend any money on the building while the local authority considered the responsibility lay elsewhere than with them. In the meantime, live bands and dancing as well as roller skating each took their turn in the ballroom. The roller skating closed in the mid-1950s but reopened a few years later under new management, playing all of the latest hits for the skaters to skate to but closed again in the 1960s. At times during the era of the roller skating, the South and the North Chambers were used as toilets; the ladies on the left consisted of three buckets each topped with a wooden seat. Also during this period, uncorroborated stories tell of swords and other weaponry being taken from the subterranean apartment and played with by local children until stolen by others.

Mr E.W. Paddick, the Hoddesdon curator and librarian, and a member of the Rye House Committee that oversaw the spending of the preservation fund, had by 1955, with others, removed yet more ivy from the walls and partially cleaned out the moat. Indeed, Mr Paddick and Mr Moodey, the Honorary Secretary of the EHAS, were extremely active in their pursuit of saving the Gatehouse from complete ruin. It had been their hope that Hertfordshire County Council would purchase the building and spend money on properly restoring it. By 1958-9, those that had campaigned for the building's survival had their efforts rewarded by receiving an assurance from Herts County Council that, with a budget of £8,000, they would restore the building and lay out the grounds with the intention of opening them to the public. The County Architect had visited the site and proposed the following recommendations: repoint the walls and make good so that no further deterioration could take place; clear the site; remove the ballroom and outbuildings, and remove the extension; clear the undergrowth and clear out the moat. Indeed, a photograph from 1959 shows the south-eastern arm of the moat by the ruinous arch, clogged with vegetation, whilst the north-eastern arm looks to be completely infilled.

At this time, the Gatehouse was owned by a Mr L.H. Lawrence who also owned the speedway and dog-racing tracks and was the licensee of the public house. Unfortunately for the campaigners and the Council, Lawrence felt that by selling the Gatehouse his plans for developing the nearby land would be hampered and so terms between them could not be met. As a consequence, the proposed works didn't come about and indeed, in 1959, Lawrence applied to develop five acres of adjoining land for industrial use. In a letter to the *Hoddesdon Journal* in July 1960, Mr Paddick describes the then-deplorable condition of the building and of the site in general. He explains how a hole in the south wall of the South Chamber had been used as a means to tip rubbish into the subterranean apartment giving the place a smell of decay and that two windows on the ground floor had either been filled in with brick or boards. (This repair to the windows, as well as the new double doors installed and a cement path laid, was to the chagrin of the EHAS who were concerned not only with the integrity of the building but also that the Council was losing interest in its purchase.) On the first floor, part of the brickwork supporting one of the oriel windows was breaking away, small trees were sprouting from the tops of these windows and also from the inner walls on the first floor (probably the same elder bushes mentioned earlier, although with additional growth), which itself was open to the weather. The extension was coming away (due to having poor or even no foundations and through not being properly bonded-in) and causing damage to the Gatehouse. On the piece of ground immediately surrounding the building was "a rather mean bungalow", some ruinous outbuildings, the remains of a van or lorry and a badly built shed that Mr Paddick thought served as a chicken house.

Soon after, the illegal "rather mean bungalow" became the subject of legal proceedings between the Council and Mr Lawrence. This put a halt to any preservation work until 1962 when all legal obstacles were removed, leading some to believe that nothing should now stop the preservation work. By 1963, due to Mr Lawrence's continued reluctance to sell the building for economic reasons, the Council had still not purchased the building nor had they done so by the following year. Nevertheless, the stone doorway had been lime washed and most of the encroaching vegetation had been removed; the moat however received little attention and remained choked with vegetation.

In an interesting letter to Mr Paddick from a member of the public dated 1965, we learn that the Gatehouse had been purchased by two retired showmen and that alarmingly the brickwork continued to crumble. Then from a letter dated April 1970, a further writer bemoans the dilapidated state of the Gatehouse which "stands on land apparently owned by Showmen who use the surrounding area as a headquarters." This would correspond with what a visitor to the Gatehouse from the Showmen's Guild Caravan Park (the former site of the fairground during the Pleasure Garden era) mentioned with regard to his uncle having owned the Gatehouse and Moated Enclosure prior to selling it to the Lee Valley Regional Park Authority.

In 1970, the main entrance was an open doorway. A notice warning people that if they entered they'd be prosecuted was attached to a section of it; but very soon after the Gatehouse was bought by the Lee Valley Regional Park Authority. The area was relieved of the accumulated tumbledown buildings, including the ballroom and the remains of the Retainers' Hall, which left the Gatehouse standing alone. With a contribution of 20 per cent from the Department of the Environment towards the cost, the restoration works began: a temporary flat roof was fitted and the eastern arm of the moat was dug out; the Victorian extension was demolished and the remains of the original curtain wall strengthened and squared off. Two new suspended pre-cast concrete floors were lowered into position, the first in the South Chamber and then at first-floor level to protect and preserve the remainder of the brick vaulting. This was then asphalted and rainwater pipes installed inside the building. Beforehand, the removal of a recent tile mosaic from what remained of the floor revealed some original floor tiles. Additional improvements included new doors to the front and rear of the Gatehouse; a new grille (gate) to the roof and a new balustrade and viewing platform; new timber windows for the ground-floor left-front and rear windows; a new delta metal grille for the first-floor south-facing window and new crenellation above the left oriel window. Other work involved the bricking-up of the hole in the rear of the fireplace, the arched hole in the south wall and the doorway in the north wall which led into the Victorian extension. Visitors to the Gatehouse throughout the 1970s remember it as having a sparse interior and being charged five new pence to enter by a man who looked seasonably cold on the door.

From 1973 until 2002 when the new visitor centre was built, the entrance to the RSPB Rye Meads Nature Reserve was north of the existing Gatehouse car park. Also during this time, a portakabin used as an office and visitor centre was located north-west of the car park on ground near to or in part previously occupied by the Maltings or Retainers' Hall.

Two photographs from 1981 show the window on the south wall open to the elements as indeed were the two small windows which follow the route of the spiral stair. Thereafter, during the 1980s and into the 1990s, further works were carried out on the building and on the enhancement of the visitor experience. Consequently, a new flat roof was fitted and positioned higher on a newly installed parapet; new metal grille windows with clear PVC sheet and opening vents were fitted; electric lighting and display panels on both floors were installed; the chimney was reconstructed with a reinstated flue; new direction boards were added at the tower, along with a new metal grille on the first-floor northern doorway; the door surround was painted with lime wash and a new reception and information desk were fitted. In addition, lime mortar was used for any necessary repointing and any badly eroded brickwork was replaced. In the main, the bricks used in the restoration came from fishermen's cottages in Great Yarmouth that were being demolished. These were the nearest in colour that could be found but had to be cut down to a thickness of two inches. Approximately 500 were needed and many were shaped by hand to fit the mullions, transoms and sills of the windows.

On the 25th April 1989, the Gatehouse was officially reopened to the public by Lord Montagu of Beaulieu, the Chairman of English Heritage. In 1995, further work was required to repair cracks that had appeared in the building. In July 2016, a ground-penetrating radar survey was undertaken at the Rye House. The results produced some interesting finds that have been mostly explored in the chapter 'From the Beginning', with the added certainty that the Moated Enclosure in particular "is not empty of archaeology."

With the assistance of Historic England, which acts in an advisory capacity, the building continues to be monitored and is very much treasured.

4. THE RYE HOUSE PLOT

The Rye House Plot or, as the pamphlets of the day put it, the "Horrid Phanatical Whiggish Plot" was a plan to assassinate King Charles II and the Duke of York. On the 1st April 1683, the King and his brother James, Duke of York ('Dismal Jimmy') were expected to return to London from Newmarket where they'd been attending the races. It was assumed that their route would take them via the "privy way" (as Pepys in May 1668 described the toll road that bypassed the Rye House). Under normal circumstances, "avoiding the bad way of the forest" (Epping) with its hidden dangers would have been a shrewd move but not on this occasion when, allegedly, there was a troop of 40 men bent on their destruction. As the royal party approached the Rye House, it would have passed through a toll gate and then, after negotiating a yard, a field and another gate, reached the narrow passage, "where two coaches at that time could not go abreast."

The plan was to overturn a farm wagon to block their way here. A party of horsemen concealed in the outer courtyard would then exit through the gate in the east wall (although another account has the horsemen hiding in a nearby copse) to come up behind and thus trap the royal party. This part of the road can be clearly seen on the Plan and Elevation (1685). The road here was bordered on one side by a high hedge and ditch and on the other by Fallowes Row.

In the meantime, further assassins with muskets, pistols and blunderbusses were to be positioned behind the nearby hedge; although in another account the assassins were to have fired through the windows of Fallowes Row or, from yet another account, the first floor of the Gatehouse. Fortunately for the King, although not for its inhabitants, there was a fire at Newmarket that destroyed half of the town and so he returned to London on the 22nd March with his brother and five Life Guards, several days earlier than expected. Thus was the plot undone.

The above outlines the plan of the conspirators; but why should there have been a plot to assassinate King Charles and his brother?

True, it was a period of turbulence with great unease concerning the excesses of the King and his court, which revived thoughts of republicanism; but was this malaise enough to induce people to commit treason? If not, could deeper motives have contributed to any unrest which promoted a plot or plots? Or was the evidence against some of those implicated in a so-called 'Rye House Plot' fabricated to enable the King to rid himself of his enemies, eliminating those who opposed his political and religious preferences?

In 1649, King Charles I was executed and England became a republic, remaining so until 1659 when Richard Cromwell ('Tumbledown Dick'), the son of Oliver Cromwell, resigned. In 1660, General Monk, the Commonwealth commander in Scotland, invited Prince Charles to return as Charles II, on condition that he wouldn't favour absolutism as his father had. Before this, Prince Charles had twice been defeated by Oliver Cromwell in battle, at Dunbar in 1650 and Worcester in 1651. After this last defeat he had escaped to the continent where he remained in exile, in France, the Dutch Republic and the Spanish Southern Netherlands.

In 1670 Charles made the Secret Treaty of Dover with Louis XIV of France, promising to declare himself a Catholic, restore Catholicism in England and support Louis against the Dutch. Louis agreed to help Charles with money and, if necessary, troops. During this time, Charles bribed certain MPs who became known as Tories (see below). It has, however, been argued, mainly by proponents of the Stuarts, that Charles never intended to declare himself a Catholic, at least not until he lay dying. He feared the uproar and repercussions of such a declaration would have been too calamitous.

In 1672, Charles suspended all laws against Catholics and joined with Louis in attacking Holland. In 1673, Charles asked Parliament for money and was compelled to accept the Test Act, which excluded all Catholics from office, and also to end war with Holland. In 1678, the 'Popish Plot' to restore Catholicism in England was announced by Titus Oates, having been fabricated as a means of promoting the Exclusion Bill.

In 1679, the Earl of Shaftesbury, leader of the Whigs, introduced the Exclusion Bill. James had refused to sign the Test Act, prompting fears that, as a Catholic, he would reign like Louis as an absolutist. The Exclusion Bill would prevent James from becoming king. Successive parliaments introduced the Bill but each time Charles dissolved them, labelling the petitioners (or Whigs, as they would become known) as subversives and closet nonconformists. In the Exclusion Bill Parliament of 1680, it was passed in the Commons but defeated in the House of Lords. It has been argued that although Charles favoured absolutism, he knew that a return to Catholicism (which would have been the consequence of this) was untenable in England; whereas James favoured both absolutism and Catholicism in equal measure. Incidentally, it was during the Exclusion Crisis that the terms 'Whig' and 'Tory' to describe someone's political and religious bent were first used. They are terms of abuse: 'Whig' implies cattle driver or horse thief; 'Tory' implies papist robber. In addition, Whig party members were supporters of protestant dissent while Tory Party members were high Anglican.

It would seem that, from 1670 onwards, the above events in history had religion at their core. There was a fear of a return to Catholicism that, when combined with absolutism, grew to become uppermost in some influential as well as some not-so-influential minds.

Richard Rumbold, the tenant of the Rye House who married the widow of a maltster and carried on business there, has been labelled as one of the principals of the Rye House Plot, if not the instigator. He was a nonconformist who had refused to obey the Act of Uniformity of 1662, which made Puritan acts of worship illegal. In addition, he'd been a guard during the execution of Charles I and had fought as a soldier in Fairfax's army during the Civil War and under Cromwell at Dunbar in 1650 and Worcester in 1651. He was a staunch republican who came to favour a combined monarchical and parliamentary system as long as it was fair and just, and was "known by the nickname of Hannibal from his having only one eye." Thus the Rye House with its republican, dissenting tenant was, it would seem, the ideal place to instigate such a plot.

More illustrious personages implicated in the plot were: the Duke of Monmouth (Charles II's eldest illegitimate son, nicknamed 'Prince Perkin' by Nell Gwynne); Lord Russell, MP for Tavistock and Bedfordshire; the Earl of Essex; Algernon Sydney; John Hampden; Lord Howard of Escrick – these formed the 'Council of Six' – and, at a later date, Lord Grey of Werke. These men were supporters of the Exclusion Bill and this, along with their subsequent clandestine meetings, led to their downfall. The Duke of Monmouth was a protestant who'd nurtured designs on becoming king. This was encouraged by Charles, who treated him like a royal prince by allowing him to wear purple, the colour of princes, and to remain hatted when others were uncovered. Moreover, it is said that Monmouth believed in a story that claimed that Charles had secretly married his mother, Lucy Walters, thereby making him Prince of Wales. This Charles flatly denied.

Those implicated who were less eminent included: Sir Thomas Armstrong, MP for Stafford; Colonel Rumsey (an old republican officer); Lieutenant Colonel Walcot (another old republican officer); Goodenough (Under Sheriff of London); Keeling (another spelling has it as 'Keiling'); West; Ferguson; and Shepard (a London wine merchant). The guide book from 1925 has it that Shepard was the occupier of the nearby King's Arms, at which meetings were held. It also claims that the details of the Plot were finally decided upon at a meeting held at the Rye House "presided over by Rumbold". Sprat (1685) states that a meeting was held in a house occupied by Shepard but makes no mention of it being a tavern near to the Rye House. On the second claim, however, Lydekker (1909) writes that "The Rye House Plot was so called from the meeting-place of the conspirators" – although this statement does rather lose some of its credibility when he adds "at Broxbourne". It is the distance from London and its coffee houses and taverns that, according to some historians, makes these Hertfordshire locations unlikely places to meet. In London, the Mitre Tavern near Aldgate and the Dolphin behind the exchange have been named as venues at which the Plot was discussed.

With the early return of the royal party, one of the conspirators, Keeling, became concerned that the Plot would come to the attention of the authorities and thought to purchase a pardon by revealing it. He took his revelations to Lord Dartmouth who referred him to Secretary Jenkins, who required a further witness for him to act. Keeling then induced his brother John, a turner from Blackfriars, to act in this capacity, which was enough for Jenkins to take action. A short time later, suffering from remorse, John Keeling informed Goodenough of their actions, suggesting they "fly beyond the sea." Many of the conspirators took to hiding including the lawyer, West, a leading figure in the conspiracy, and Colonel Rumsey; but eventually both handed themselves in and confessed. These two along with Ferguson the Plotter, a Presbyterian Minister and later Chaplain General to the forces in Monmouth's Rebellion of 1685, had been overheard threatening to "lop the King and the Duke of York." West and Rumsey, now alarmed for their safety, turned against their accomplices and stated that Walcot had been appointed as the commander of the troop to assassinate the King and Duke, and further swore that Rumbold had offered his house to assist the 40 men whose task it was to carry out the deed. Upon Rumsey's evidence and Shepard's confession, orders were issued for the arrests of the 'great men'.

The Duke of Monmouth absconded but, as he was a particular favourite of the King's, little time and effort were spent on finding him. Nevertheless, Lord Halifax prevailed upon the Duke to write two letters of submission to the King and, having done so, because of their relationship Monmouth was invited to attend the Court and there make his confession. This he duly did and obtained his pardon, only to go back on his word (see below). The King was furious and so banished him from the kingdom to the United Provinces (the Dutch Republic). He returned in 1685 after Charles's death in an attempt to seize the throne from James II at the Battle of Sedgemoor. He was captured – indeed, he was dragged crying from a ditch – imprisoned and, in an attempt to save his life, offered to convert to Catholicism. Within two days he was beheaded on Tower Hill. At his execution, he made a request to the executioner not to make two blows of the axe, as with poor Russell – although another account states that it took three strokes to finish Russell, even though he had just paid the executioner ten guineas. However, the axe was raised and then feebly let fall onto his neck. After this, Monmouth reprovingly raised his head to gently replace it. In all it took five blows of the axe to sever his head.

Of the remaining members of the Council of Six, Lord Russell, Algernon Sydney and Essex were imprisoned; and the latter killed himself by cutting his throat. At the time, murder was suspected but Gilbert Burnet (1643-1715) (also known as Bishop Burnet), a Scottish philosopher and historian who knew Essex well, accepted that he died by his own hand saying that Essex had spoken of suicide as an honourable course. Indeed, Essex had asked his servant for a penknife to "pare his nails" but, finding it impossible, had said that a razor would suffice. Nevertheless, the rumours that the government was behind his murder continued to grow, forcing the government to bring to trial on 2nd February 1684 the two lawyers who had helped spread such reports. But even this didn't placate the rumours, which eventually led to the writing of *A True Account...* by Thomas Sprat in 1685.

Lord Russell and Algernon Sydney were later beheaded on the evidence of Lord Howard who had turned informer in the hope of saving himself. It was during Russell's trial that the news that Essex had committed suicide by cutting his own throat with the razor was announced. Apparently, Lord Russell became greatly agitated upon hearing this, which George Jeffreys – later to be known as the infamous Judge Jeffreys, he of the 'bloody assize' – who was leading the prosecution at the trial, took as confirmation of his guilt. Some historians argue that Lord Russell was executed as revenge for the death in 1680 of Lord Stafford who had opposed the

Exclusion Bill and whose death had been forced by the supporters of the Bill.

At the trial of Algernon Sydney, Lord Howard was the only witness against him. It was presided over by the newly promoted Judge Jeffreys after the dismissal of Sir Francis Pemberton, who had been the judge at the trial of Lord Russell and who'd favoured Russell's innocence. The law required there to be two witnesses for treason. A book was produced which Sydney had written against tyranny some years earlier and this was used as the second witness, even though the book had no bearing on the case. Nevertheless, Judge Jeffreys decided that "scribere est agere" - to write is to act.

John Hampden was convicted not of treason but of high misdemeanour, imprisoned and fined £40,000. Beforehand, the Duke of York had summoned Monmouth to corroborate the evidence of Howard, which he refused to do. Consequently, the evidence to convict Hampden was the same as that used to sentence and execute Sydney. The opinion of the diarist Evelyn, who credited Sydney with having had "some bloody designe to set up a commonwealth and turn all things topsy turvy", is somewhat condemning in thought; but in truth, by 1684, after a long succession of convictions the acquittal of Joseph Hayes, who was accused of sending money to Holland to aid the conspirators, indicates that the desire for retribution was waning. According to Gilbert Burnet, this shows that juries were again asserting their independence, no longer being prepared to return verdicts as instructed by Judge Jeffreys. The exuberance shown in reaction to the King and his brother surviving an assassination attempt was wearing thin - as thin, it would seem, as the evidence against some of those implicated in the Plot.

Lord Howard was pardoned.

The fates of the other conspirators were mixed. Richard Rumbold fled to Holland. Because he had informed Leoline Jenkins, Secretary of State for the Southern Department (this was a position in Cabinet, which after 1782 became the Foreign Office), Keeling was granted a pardon; as too were Rumsey and West in December 1684. Ferguson the Plotter having escaped to Holland then became instrumental, or so it is said he would have people believe, in persuading Monmouth to invade England in 1685. After the failure at Sedgemoor, he managed to escape arrest and in that year was pardoned by King James II. The reason for this is not certain although some have suggested that James was grateful to Ferguson for having led Monmouth into a trap. Having gained a free pardon, he then transferred his loyalty to the Prince of Orange. But he wasn't finished plotting because, once William was on the throne, Ferguson began to oppose him. He died in 1714.

Sir Thomas Armstrong and Colonel Thomas Walcot were convicted of High Treason and were hanged, drawn and quartered. The fate of Thomas Armstrong's head has been outlined in the chapter 'The Gatehouse and the Moated Enclosure'. Walcot's head was displayed on Aldgate, although his quarters were buried. Walcot, incidentally, was against the assassination of the royal party.

There is some confusion amongst historians as to what the term 'drawn' means in this instance. To some, because 'drawn' follows 'hanged', the former implies that the victim is disembowelled and his intestines are drawn out. (A male pronoun is used here because the sentence for a woman found guilty of high treason was to be burned at the stake; although by royal command this could be substituted with beheading, usually if the person sentenced was royal or of the nobility.) To others, 'drawn' merely implies that the victim is tied to a wooden hurdle or board and drawn by a horse to his place of execution. Those who support the former view consider that to be hanged, drawn and quartered is to undergo the events in sequence, whereas those who oppose this view consider that 'drawn' follows 'hung' because being drawn behind a horse is only a supplementary part of the sentence. When you consider that the hanging here was not to death but rather only to a point very near to death; and that the victim was then taken down to undergo the remainder of the sentence (emasculation, disembowelling, beheading and the body finally being chopped into quarters), it's easy to see what they mean. However, in Sprat (1685, p.160) the sentence for High Treason is described as drawing, hanging and quartering.

Two conflicting accounts also have Richard Rumbold's head placed on a spike but in different places. One has it over the entrance (the triangular block) while another on a spike on the barley twist chimney; but this would have been in the year 1685 after he'd returned to take part in Argyll's Rising. He'd been badly wounded in hand-to-hand fighting and received a traitor's death in Edinburgh. One of his quarters was exhibited at Aldgate, London and another on one of the aforementioned spikes at the top of the Gatehouse. Although according to another account, his limbs were suspended from a nearby elm tree. To add to the confusion, in a further account the exhibiting of one of his quarters at the Gatehouse was considered doubtful. From warrants dated the 27th and 28th October 1685 it is understood that one quarter of his body was to be set up on Aldgate whilst the remaining three quarters were to be placed at or near the Rye House, Hoddesdon, the Rye, and Bishops Stortford. Such documents therefore confirm the destination of some of his remains, but not their precise location.

The Plot Discussed

As we know it today in its simplistic form, the Plot consists of all of the above elements. Leading Whigs who supported Exclusion were implicated in the Plot and were removed from the political scene. At a time when civil and religious liberties were under threat from a monarch with absolutist tendencies, anathema to all with republican sympathies, and where James, a Catholic, had been named as successor, in an era of discontent, a plot or plots were in existence. This is strongly supported by a contemporary writer who considered that there were those "who must have plots to make their services necessary, and have an interest to keep them alive" – and moreover, by the Duke of Monmouth admitting in a letter to the King as having had "so great a share in the other part of the said conspiracy". But whether all of those implicated were deeply involved in a plot to assassinate the King and his brother is doubtful. Indeed, the Duke of Monmouth was distraught that the King should think him capable of doing him harm. He went back on his word, not over this matter, but because he then found himself disgraced with his party, the Whigs. But was there ever a Rye House Plot or was it just an idea?

The *Antipapists* by Savage, John. Political anti-Catholic joint portrait of seven figures of the Rye House Plot with Edward Berry Godfrey (connected with the Popish Plot).

As mentioned above, it is argued that both Charles and James favoured absolutism. The King's failure to summon Parliament in 1684, as he was bound by the Triennial Act, does support this claim whilst his disdain for such an auspicious gathering is emphasised by the simple act of tossing his handkerchief in the air declaring: "I care just that for Parliament." As for James, his strong influence over Charles is recorded in the Duke of Monmouth's journal where he writes that the King was "inclined to save the Lord Russel but was forced to consent otherwise he must have broke with his brother." Here then was an opportunity for the Stuarts to rid themselves not only of leading Whigs but also of some leading participants who had opposed their father during the English Civil War: Walcot, Armstrong and Richard Rumbold. In Rumbold's case, however, they had to wait until 1685 when he returned to join Argyll's rising. He was wounded, captured and, after a minimal trial, executed the same afternoon. While on the scaffold he admitted to being horrified at the notion of "destroying the King and his brother" and further spoke out against popery and absolutism. A righteous man who went on to say "for none comes into the world with a saddle on his back, neither any man booted or spurred to ride him" – words that resonate to this day. He was called a "confounded villain" by a Scotch [Scots] Privy Councillor to which he answered: "I am at peace with God, how then can I be confounded?" In an age when Christianity played such an important part in the lives of individuals, it seems strange that a devout man would lie as he was about to meet his maker.

That said, Gilbert Burnet wrote that Rumbold had informed the conspirators that he had a house at Hoddesdon that the King would pass on his way to and from Newmarket. It is also claimed that at one of the two meetings he said to the conspirators: "Once the coach went through alone without any of the guards about it." Adding that by blocking the road he could have shot them both. These accounts don't seem to compare with his words from the scaffold – but is fleeing the country the action of an innocent man? Dixon (1871) is of the opinion that he had offered "house and horse" to the cause but remained unaware of the assassination plot and was intent instead upon "an open fight". A reasoning, as a soldier, that is perhaps more in tune with his scaffold confession. Rumbold aside, Burnet then added: "upon which they [the conspirators] ran into much wicked talk about the way of executing their design. But nothing was ever fixed, all was but idle talk." In addition, a further contemporary historian, David Hume, the Apologist for the Stuarts, surprisingly wrote: "the scheme gave great pleasure to the conspirators, no concerted design was yet laid; nor any men, horses, or arms provided. The whole was little more than loose discourse, the overflowing of their zeal and rancour."

All of the above has helped to fuel the belief that it was the idea of the Rye House Plot that was used as a means – some say more by the Catholic Duke of York and his supporters than by the King – to discredit the Whig Party and destroy its protestant leaders. Just as the 'Popish Plot' was fabricated to discredit the Tories and exclude James from the succession. Catholicism and absolutism were at the core of any unrest and encompassed those seeking to plot and those who considered themselves plotted against, while a return to republicanism, although uppermost in some minds, West's included, was not wholeheartedly embraced. Richard Rumbold, a staunch republican, for example advocated a combination of the monarchical system with Parliament. Any evidence against the 'Six' with regard to the Rye House Plot was weak to say the least and most of the testimony by the informers has been proved to be mere tales. Indeed, according to Burnet, the evidence of West and Rumsey was so improbable that it wasn't worth publishing. Another account considers that "[t]he Conspirators were of an inferior order who held frequent meetings quite unknown to Monmouth and the Cabal of six." Within the pages of Sprat (1685) we find the assertion that "[b]oth Charles and James had made divers [some or various] alterations to the text" in an attempt, it would seem, to make good their actions.

In conclusion, we shall never know the absolute truth; but from what has been presented above, the Rye House Plot would seem to have been an idea only, the idea of a few that, in the end, was used to condemn a host of discontented people. That is not to imply that some of those put to death or implicated were completely innocent in thought or deed; but then that's another story, a story not of assassination but rather of something alluded to by Monmouth as "the other part of the said conspiracy": insurrection!

5. THE GREAT BED OF WARE

Apart from one year between April 2012 and the following April when the Great Bed returned to Ware to go on display at the local museum, it has resided at the Victoria and Albert Museum in London since 1931. The bed is of interest not only because of its size but also for its literary associations and as a piece of furniture history.

The Great Bed consists of 40 separate components and weighs 641 kg. "The over-all width of the structure is 10 feet 7 inches, the length is 10 feet 10 inches and the height is 8 feet 9 inches" (Thornton, 1976). It is believed at one time to have been higher but was cut down to fit the room given over to it at the Saracens Head in Ware,

The Great Bed of Ware.

Hertfordshire. A Swiss traveller, Cesar de Saussure, who toured parts of Hertfordshire in 1728 claimed the Bed was so high that steps were needed to get into it. Other accounts greatly rejoiced in the Great Bed's size by saying that it could "hold twenty couples" while another stated that "26 butchers and their wives" had slept in the bed on the night of King William III's coronation. Its impressive nature and size emphasise that it's better seen than described; but for those unable to do so, Cussans (1870) gives a fairly good description: "the massive posts are plain at the bottom, and at about 2 feet from the ground are four pillars one at each angle of the posts. These pillars support four arches, above which the posts, elaborately carved, continue for about 4 feet more; the total height being about 8 feet. The canopy and the head of the bed are finely carved, the latter, with human figures, fluted work, heraldic roses and gothic arches". The Great Bed is of oak (wainscot) while the carved areas were originally painted. Because of this and the inlaid work (marquetry) set into the headboard, which at the time of its construction was new to England, it is of interest to furniture historians. In addition, to this day it has waxed seals of nobles adorning the headboard and bedposts as well as graffiti carved into the woodwork by people Cussans terms "idle sightseers". In its day it would also have had colourful curtains and cornices adorning it that it is believed were more costly to produce than the Great Bed itself!

The V&A considers the Great Bed to have been made between 1590 and 1600. This would make it Elizabethan and indeed the style of carving is consistent with that period. They attribute the design to one Hans Vredeman de Vries (1527-1604) and think that it was probably made in Ware - although the inlay work was most probably carried out by Rhenish inlay workers then established in Southwark. On the back of the headboard, however, is painted the date 1463.

This was the time of Edward IV, for whom, it has been claimed, the Great Bed was made by an artisan named Jonas Fosbrooke. Supposedly, it took him 30 years and the King was so impressed with the outcome that he gave Fosbrooke a pension of 40 marks a year. It is also claimed that it was made for the Earl of Warwick known as the Kingmaker. What we can believe is that the painted date is more modern than the year it represents. This would suggest perhaps that the year 1463 was added in an attempt to authenticate its age and enhance its desirability and market value. Incidentally, Ware Park was formerly the property of Warwick and indeed an unearthed escutcheon bearing his badge was found in the grounds.

Another topic of interest concerning the Great Bed involves the paranormal activity once associated with it. Apparently, the ghost of Jonas Fosbrooke was inclined to keep sleepers awake by pinching, nipping and scratching. He was vexed at the base and common use of the bed he'd made for royalty. This occurred more than once and consequently the Great Bed gained a reputation. Perhaps a more understandable explanation for all of that pinching, nipping and scratching can be gleaned from a newspaper article in which the writer attributed such activity to fleas. Nevertheless, there were those who agreed with Fosbrooke's sentiment concerning the Great Bed's ill use. The county historian Sir Henry Chauncy, writing in 1700, tells a story about six Londoners and their wives who went to Ware "on a Frolick." Their intention was to sleep six at the top and six at the bottom with no man near any woman other than his wife. The idea was to have one man and two women then two men and one woman and so on, with the sixth man on the outside like the first. The landlord discovering their intent decided to add a little spice of his own to their posset (hot milk curdled with ale or wine with added spices) resulting in them being incommoded all night, which left little time for any sort of pinching, nipping or scratching!

Another story set *before* the Great Bed's actual date of manufacture (according to the V&A) involves Henry VIII! His Lancashire Master of Horse, a Mr Harrison Daxby, took a liking to the daughter of a miller and maltster residing at Chalk Island, near Ware. This came to the attention of the King as he made his way to Hertford. He gathered the girl and all her suitors and offered her hand to the man who would spend the night in the Great Bed and be found there in the morning. Being of a superstitious nature, the suitors declined to do so but the Master of the Horse was made of stronger stuff. He was found the next morning on the floor covered in bruises and in a state of exhaustion; and, so the story goes, thus he won her hand.

Henry continues to be associated with the Great Bed both through its connection with Nonsuch Palace and also because it is claimed he gave it to the Fanshawe family in recognition of their assistance in uniting the red and white roses. Another account from Johnson (1952) again involving the Fanshawe family recognises that it was made during Elizabeth's reign but claims the Bed was left behind at the manor house to be sold when Thomas Fanshawe moved in 1575 to a newly built mansion at Ware Park. The manor house in this instance was Place House where the Fanshawe family had lived since 1570. Indeed, Johnson is adamant that the Bed had belonged to Thomas Fanshawe. That said, as to whether the period from 1558, at the beginning of Elizabeth's reign, to 1575 falls in the category "cannot have been made much before 1590" is unclear but, for reasons of style alone, it is believed to be unlikely. This raises the possibility that a similarly large bed housed at Place House was left behind to be sold at a later date and was then wrongly assumed to be the Great Bed of Ware. Indeed, Paul Hentzner of Brandenburg, travelling in England later in Elizabeth's reign, informs us that the beds of the nobility and even those of farmers were made for show with tapestries, carvings and hangings.

A further theory has it that the Bed was moved from Ware Park to a local inn between 1590 and 1596. Again, it is considered unlikely that the owners would keep it for only a few years, given the expense involved in its manufacture; or was it sold at Ware Park, but at a later date? On the death of Henry Fanshawe in 1616, the bed and furniture of the 'best chamber' were bequeathed to his wife who in turn bequeathed bedstead, feather bed and bolster to her son on her death in 1631. In an article by W.F. Andrews, founder member of the East Herts Archaeological Society, it is suggested that this was possibly the Great Bed; if so, any sale could not have taken place until 1631 or after. Ware Park, incidentally, was sold by the Fanshawes in 1667! In truth, the history of the Bed is shrouded in conjecture: indeed, after much diligent enquiry, the Hertfordshire historian Robert Clutterbuck (1827) couldn't unearth any documents in connection with it! As a consequence, all of the above contributes only colour to its history, whilst also being a tad bewildering.

The modern theory is inclined to see the Great Bed as having been purposefully made as a tourist attraction for an inn. Using the Lumley inventories from 1590 (a documentation of paintings, furniture, etc. compiled by John 1st Baron Lumley, 1533–1609), Thornton (1976) considers it not to have been of the top class and, at best, only "middling grand". Beds were listed as: "Bedsteades gylt iiii (4) Bedsteades of walnutree and markatre xxiii (23) Bedsteades of weynskot xl (40)". This would mean that it "falls between the second and third Lumley categories" (Thornton, 1976) and so is hardly likely to have been made for a grand house. In short, it is its size that has made it famous, not its quality! To support this theory, by 1600 the Great Bed was notorious enough for Shakespeare to include it in his play, *Twelfth Night*, which would seem to suggest that it had been used by the many rather than by a few visitors to a stately home. Further, Ware was only a day's journey from London by the old North Road and the number of people passing through must have been quite considerable. Consequently, as the waxed seals would seem to indicate, it was necessary to cater for all tiers of society. Indeed, in 1596, a royal German visitor by the name of Prince Ludwig of Anhalt-Kohten spent the night in what is thought to have been the Crown (though some doubt this, even though it was the principal inn of Ware at that time) in a bed described in his *Poetical Itinerary* in the following manner: "At Ware was a bed of dimensions so wide, Four couples might cosily lie side by side, And thus without touching each other abide." With such a description, it is quite natural to presume that he was alluding to the Great Bed. Incidentally, Cussans (1870) claims that the Bed was originally in the Crown Inn.

It is believed that the next recorded sleeper occupied the Bed in 1610, a Ludwig Friedrich of Wurttemberg – yet another German Prince. From the diary of a friend of the Prince, this: "I slept in a bed of Swan's down 8 feet wide." It is believed that the author is referring to his master and, although this is interesting in itself, a bed 8 feet wide is 2 feet 7 inches narrower than the Great Bed. This is far from conclusive evidence but the assumption is that the bed in question was the Great Bed. If this was the case and if, moreover, the Great Bed initially *was* at the Crown, then it would seem that between the two dates the Bed had been moved because the Prince's secretary records that the particular night in question was spent at the Stag. It is assumed that he was referring to the White Hart, where it remained until 1706 when it was moved to the George. It was subsequently moved (or was this a return move?) to the Crown, where it remained until 1765 when the inn was demolished. From then on, reports of its whereabouts and ownership are conflicting. Some accounts have it moved to the Saracens Head whilst others have it transferred first to the Bull Inn and then to the Saracens Head.

Cussans (1870) was of the opinion that the Great Bed was moved to the Bull Inn while, from a *Glossary by Nares* dated about 1820, the conclusion at this time was that the Great Bed still remained in the Bull Inn. In an undated letter to the *Hertfordshire Mercury*, a local resident describes an incident that although occurring several years later is nevertheless connected with the Bull Inn. He writes that old Fanny Brown, as the last licensee of the Bull Inn in the High Street opposite the Old Town Hall, was disappointed when Queen Victoria and Prince Albert shortly after they were married didn't leave their coach for refreshment as arranged when passing through Ware. This testimony suggests that the Great Bed was the attraction here – although it could have been Fanny Brown – and that Victoria and Albert's visit to the Bull was so arranged because of its presence. Soon after, 'old Fanny Brown' removed from the Bull Inn to a cottage on London Road; whereas the Great Bed, it would seem, went to the Saracens Head.

There it remained for a time, until the same local resident tells us: "[I was] present at the Saracens Head in 1864 when a Mr Willmott of Hertford bid £100. No one else bid and upon it being knocked down and the auctioneer inquiring of the name, Mr Willmott answered Charles Dickens but I do not know if the bid was genuine. I only know that shortly afterwards it was removed away." It is hard to refute such testimony, even if, as claimed by some, Dickens only tried to buy the Bed; but the affirmation declaring that it was taken away, although illuminating, is by no means definitive. Or is it? From the publication, *England as Seen by Foreigners*, this: "In September 1864 the famous Shakespeare bed was sold by auction and purchased for 100 guineas for Mr Charles Dickens and is now, we believe, at Gad's Hill, a famous Shakespearian locality." (p.212) Also of interest is the significance of the name Willmott. Although spelt differently, Wilmot was the name of the aristocrat played by Dickens in an amateur production in which his good friend Wilkie Collins played his valet. That surely then is the end of the matter: the above accounts offer irrefutable evidence; but a Mr Charles Whitley Jun from Hoddesdon was also present at the auction at the Saracens Head and claims that no one advanced upon the bid of 100 guineas, that it was not sold to Charles Dickens and, further to making enquiries, claims it remained at the Saracens Head!

Perhaps, instead, the following from a writer who claimed he saw the sale of effects at the Saracens Head in 1864 will help. He writes that the bed was bought by Mr W.H. Teale in that year who also purchased the tapestry and carved fittings formerly in the same room with the bedstead. Yet even this testimony is contradicted. W.F. Andrews writes that the sale of effects at the Saracens Head in 1864 saw the Great Bed bought at auction for a small sum, but then adds that shortly afterwards it was bought by Teale for a "considerable amount". Unfortunately, he doesn't say from whom or from where, or whether this was by auction. A letter dated 30th May 1870 written on Rye House paper at Rye House and signed Jackson & Son inexplicably has the name of Teale in the left-hand bottom corner and informs the recipient that he is "at full liberty to take the Great Bed of Ware away when you feel disposed." Again, this is all very bewildering. What the evidence does suggest, however, is that the Bed was in the ownership of the Teale family by 1870, which incidentally was also the year of Dickens' death!

Where was the Bed housed? In an undated article, W.F. Andrews writes that it was "removed from an old building to a commodious new building expressly erected for it". The 'new building', as shown on the Freehold for Sale Map from 1881, was positioned at the east end of the Long Walk. A newspaper article from 1883 also places the new building, known as the Great Bed House, at the same location. Moving on to 1898, *Bygone Hertfordshire* (edited by W. Andrews) states that: "The present resting place of this unique piece of furniture is the Rye House Inn" which is rather odd because the guide book of that year was waxing lyrical about the "commodious new building" – although as with the topic of the 'subterranean passage' mentioned in the chapter 'The Gatehouse and Moated Enclosure', the written text was inclined to be interchangeable. But Andrews is not alone in his observation because Harper (1904) writes that the Great Bed was a staple attraction at the Rye House Inn (the "gimcrack") where apparently one could also "guzzle and swill". By 1905, however, Graveson writes: "In another part of the grounds is a small building which finds accommodation for the Great Bed of Ware." This would be the "small building near the Main Gates" as mentioned in the *Guide Book* from 1925, positioned in between the footpath and the road approximately in line with the south-west angle of the Gatehouse. The Bed remained on display and in the ownership of the Teale family until 1904 when Christie & Co. of the Hoddesdon Brewery bought the estate. In 1928, it passed to the Cannon Brewery of London when Christies Brewery, which included the Gatehouse and the Great Bed, was sold. In 1931 it was sold to a Mr Frank Partridge, a London antiques dealer, for £4,000 who had it on display in his auction house with the intention of selling it on overseas. Thankfully, this didn't materialise, which resulted in him selling it in 1931 for the same amount he paid for it to the V&A where, apart from the brief visit to Ware Museum, it has remained ever since.

To this day, some believe that the Great Bed was once housed in the Gatehouse. Armitage (1948) wrote that it was part of the museum while, also from the not-too-distant past, a visitor to the Gatehouse in the 1930s wrote that "Inside one could see the Great Bed of Ware". Considering that, when the Bed was recently exhibited at the Ware Museum, parts of it had to be lowered through the roof, it's hard at first to understand this statement. But on reflection, when the number of small inns it has frequented over the years is taken into account, the possibility appears less unlikely. Meanwhile, the visitor was under the impression that the Great Bed was housed in the Gatehouse. It's feasible that at the time of his visit, the Bed had either been sold and removed, and that he mistook Queen Elizabeth's bed for it; or that the bed was still on site in the 'small building' provided and the Gatehouse was considered to be that same 'small building'. Or towards the end of its stay at Rye House, was the Great Bed indeed housed in the Gatehouse? Mr E.W. Paddick, the librarian curator of Hoddesdon, writing in the

Hertfordshire Countryside magazine in 1965, was having none of it and was firmly of the opinion that the Great Bed, before its removal in 1931, was never housed at the Gatehouse. Although also before its removal, he was further of the opinion that the Great Bed was never moved from the "commodious new building" at the east end of the Long Walk!

Photographs of the bed when at the Rye House show it with a set of antlers at its front, attached above the cornice. These relate to the ceremony named the 'Swearing of the Horns' where, for a fee, the innkeeper proclaimed a cautionary oath over the visitor. This custom was already considered to be ancient by 1706.

As for the Great Bed's literary associations, the most often quoted example is that in Shakespeare's *Twelfth Night*, Act III, scene 2, where the bed is mentioned by Sir Toby Belch as a symbol of immensity: "and as many lies as will lie in thy sheet of paper, although the sheet were big enough for the Bed of Ware". The bed is also mentioned by Ben Johnson in in his plays *The Alchemist* and *The Silent Woman*; by George Farquhar in *The Recruiting Officer*; by Byron in *Don Juan*; and by Dickens in 'The Holly Tree'.

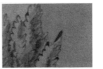

6. THE PARANORMAL

At the time of writing, the Gatehouse has stood for 574 years. Understandably, a building of such great age has become the subject of a few popular beliefs and folklore over the years, as touched upon in the chapter, 'The Gatehouse and Moated Enclosure'. Today, any paranormal activity recorded with the aid of technology may, when combined with people's personal experiences and unearthed stories, in turn become the popular belief and folklore of the future.

Since 2015, paranormal investigation teams have undertaken a number of investigations and in so doing have accumulated a range of material that along with reports of orbs, cold spots and ghostly lights also includes a photograph of an apparition. It is captured standing in profile near to the door of the south chamber and looks very much like a fifteenth-century armoured knight with a helmet similar in shape to that of a jaw-bone visor helmet or sallet. The reaction to this photograph from several personages connected with paranormal activity has been enthusiastic to say the least. It is believed that something was in an early stage of manifestation and that, because no flash was used, this something was creating its own illumination. Further material includes a video of a moving black mass both in the first-floor room and on the spiral staircase; and a non-visual experience involving a smell of burning flesh which emanated from the subterranean apartment/dungeon, rather like that of pork. As no similar smell could be detected outside of the building, it was considered to be associated with the Duke, an aggressive entity that inhabits the subterranean apartment/dungeon and the ground floor. He was given to inflicting torturous acts on people (including burning) and there have been reports of members from different teams fainting or collapsing when investigating this entity.

The apparition captured in the randomly taken photograph by Tracy Jenkins

Less demonstrative entities include Charles, a night watchman from the seventeenth century who has made himself known at every investigation. He is seen throughout the Gatehouse but especially on the spiral staircase and should be greeted on entering the building and acknowledged when leaving. Anne Parr was sister to Catherine Parr, the sixth wife of Henry VIII, who lived at the Rye House until the death of her mother in 1531. She is seen in the room on the first floor and could possibly be the 'lady in blue' described by a visitor to the Gatehouse who, upon entering, viewed just such an apparition sitting on the left-hand windowsill, to the front. Richard and Isobel Duchamp, a brother and sister, are seen very rarely and, to date, only in the first-floor room. On the occasion of my attendance at one investigation, I was informed that Isobel was holding a baby, the product of an incestuous relationship between the two.

On a more personal note, I have been involved with the Gatehouse since 2013 and during that time I've experienced no paranormal activity of a conclusive nature – unless the following can be construed as such. On a Sunday morning following the previous night's paranormal investigation, I was preparing the Gatehouse for that day's visitors. I entered the first-floor room to find it in an uncustomarily untidy condition. I can only describe what I felt as a 'shared feeling', as though the displeasure were not all my own! This may have been imagined and caused by my heightened senses because of the earlier investigation or perhaps it was indeed a shared moment. That apart, I have witnessed visitors feeling unable to enter the Gatehouse because of what they sense within; and, once inside, visitors almost immediately leaving after venturing no farther than the ground floor, uttering phrases along the lines of "there's something by that door", referring to the door to the south chamber.

Perhaps the most memorable encounter with a visitor involved an elderly gentleman from the Showmen's Ground that occupies the site of the old Fairground. He'd heard from his relatives of my intention to write a history on the Rye House and felt compelled, despite feeling unwell, to struggle over and tell me of his experience, which had occurred several years earlier. One evening he was walking his dog in the Moated Enclosure near to the northern arm of the moat when a figure dressed in a type of robe emerged from where the remains of the window and wall stand to the west. The figure approached him and the elderly gentleman made a greeting; the figure then went round to the back of a shrub – which the elderly gentlemen described as a holly bush – and disappeared. To the day he related the story, the elderly gentleman remained convinced that what he saw was an apparition.

The robe is possibly of importance here. If it was a monk he encountered, this could either be in connection with the chapel or, from a period predating the building of the house, a warrior monk of the Knights Templar or the Knights Hospitallers from the nearby Manor of Temple Roydon. At the suppression of the Knights Templars in 1313, Temple Roydon was given by Edward II to the Knights Hospitallers. And indeed, before the story with regard to the elderly gentleman was known, a warrior monk was seen by a medium within the vicinity of the Moated Enclosure, near to where the elderly gentleman encountered his apparition.

REFERENCES

Andrews, R.T. (1902) *The Rye House Castle and the Manor of Rye*, EHAST.

Andrews, R.T. (1905) 'The Rye House and its Plot', in *The Memorials of Old Hertfordshire* edited by Percy Cross Standing, London and Derby: Bemrose and Sons.

Andrews, W. (ed.) (1898) *Bygone Hertfordshire*, London: William Andrews & Co.

Anonymous (1903) *Memories of a Sister of S. Saviour's Priory*, London: A.R. Mawbray & Co. Limited.

Armitage, H., (1948) *Russell and Rye House*, Letchworth.

Buildingconservation.com, 'Tudor Brickwork', http://www.buildingconservation.com/articles/tudor-brickwork/tudor-brickwork.htm.

Clutterbuck, R. (1827) *The History and Antiquities of the County of Hertford*.

Cromwell, T. (2016) *Rye House GPR Survey Report*.

Cussans, J.E. (1870) *History of Hertfordshire, Vol. 1*, Stephen Austin & Sons.

Department of the Environment, List of Buildings of Special Architectural Interest, 1951.

Dixon, W.H. (1871) *Her Majesty's Tower, Vol. IV*, London: Hurst & Blacketh.

Emery, A. (2000) *Greater Mediaeval Houses England and Wales, 1300-1500, Vol. 2*, CUP.

Emery, A. (2006) *Greater Mediaeval Houses England and Wales 1300-1500, Vol. 3, Southern England*, CUP.

Ewald, A.E. (1885) *Rye House Plot: Historical Sketches*, Piccadilly: Chatto and Windus.

Garside, S. (2002) *Hoddesdon: A History*, Phillimore.

Gentleman's Magazine (1844) p.424.

Gentleman's Magazine (1857) p.711.

Gilmore Hankey Kirke Ltd (2010) 'Rye House Gatehouse and Quay Conservation Management Plan'.

Gover, J.E.B., Mawer, A., and Stenton, F.M. (1938) *The Place-Names of Hertfordshire*, Cambridge University Press.

Graveson, W. (1905) *Hertford and its Surroundings*, Homeland Association, Ltd.

Grose, F., *Antiquities of England and Wales*, writing in between 1783-87.

Harper, C.G. (1904) *The Newmarket, Bury, Thetford and Cromer Road*, London: Chapman & Hall Ltd.

Harvey, J.H. (1969) *The Itineraries of William Worcestre*, OUP.

Hayllar, H.F. (1948) *The Chronicles of Hoddesdon: From the Earliest Times to the Present Day*, Hoddesdon: Thomas Knight & Co.

Johnson, W.B. (1952) *Companion into Hertfordshire*, London: Methuen & Co.

Lee Valley Regional Park Authority (no date) *Rye House Gatehouse*.

Lydekker, R. (1909) *Hertfordshire*, CUP.

Lynch, G., Watt, D., and Colston, B. (2006) 'An Investigation of Hand Tools Used for English Cut-and-Rubbed and Gauged Brickwork'.

Macaulay, T.B. (1914) *The History of England from the Accession of James the Second, Vol. II*, London: Macmillan.

Mills, A.D. (1991) *Dictionary of English Place-Names*, OUP.

Milne, D.J. (1951) *Results of The Rye House Plot and their influence upon the Revolution of 1688*.

Neale, F. (2000) *The Topography of Medieval Bristol*, Bristol Record Society, Vol. 51.

Pears Encyclopaedia, fifth edition (1965).

Penny Magazine (1840).

RCHME (2000) 'Monument Details'.

Royal Commission on Historical Monuments of England (1910) *Inventory of the Historical Monuments in Hertfordshire*, HMSO.

Rumbold, Richard (1685) 'Speech on the Scaffold', http://www.bartleby.com/268/3/15.html.

Salmon, N. (1728) *History of Hertfordshire*.

Senior, W. (1877) *By Stream and Sea*, Piccadilly: Chatto & Windus.

Shaw, W.A., and King, C.T. (eds) (1911) *Letters of Denization and Acts of Naturalization of Aliens in England and Ireland*, Norwich.

Smith, J.T. (1993) *Hertfordshire Houses: Selective Inventory*.

Smith, J.T. (1992) *English Houses 1200–1800: The Hertfordshire Evidence*, RCHME.

Smith, T.P. (1975) 'Rye House, Hertfordshire, and Aspects of Early Brickwork in England', *Archaeological Journal*, Vol. 132, Royal Archaeological Institute.

Sprat, T. (1685) *A True Account and Declaration of the Horrid Conspiracy to Assassinate the Late King Charles II and the Duke of York*.

Teale, J. (1898) *A Guide to Rye House*.

Teale, W.H. (1856) *A Guide to Rye House*.

Thornton, P.K. (1976) *Victoria and Albert Museum Masterpieces*.

Tomkins, M. (2001) *So that was Hertfordshire: Travellers Jottings 1322–1887*.

Tompkins, H.W. (1902) *Highways & Byways in Hertfordshire*, New York: Macmillan and Co Limited.

Tregelles, J.A. (1908) *A History of Hoddesdon*.

Tristram, W.O. (1910) *Moated Houses*, London: Methuen & Co.

TudorHistory.org, In the Footsteps of the Six Wives of Henry VIII Blog Tour, tudorhistory.org/blog.

Victoria History of the Counties of England, The, 1912.

Vince, A.J. (1925) *An Historical Guide to The Rye House*.

Wagner, L. (1891) *Names and their Meaning*, London: G.P. Putnam's Sons.

Whitley, C., and Andrews, R.T. (1888) *A Description of the Boundaries of the Hamlet of Hoddesdon*.

Wight, J.A. (1972) *Brick Building in England from Middle Ages to 1550*, London.

Wikipedia, 'James Scott, 1st Duke of Monmouth'.

Wikipedia, 'Rye House Gatehouse'.

Wikipedia, 'The Rye House Plot'.

Winstone, B. (1889) 'Rye House, 1685', Collingridge, City Press, London.

Wood, M. (1996) *The English Mediaeval House*, London: Studio Editions, an imprint of Random House UK Ltd.

OTHER RESOURCES

bcw-project.org

British History Online

British Listed Buildings, website

Cabinet 9: Political Conspiracies, https://www.otago.ac.nz/library/exhibitions/authorship/cabinet9-3.html

FreeBMD-search, website

gatehouse-gazetteer.info

Gerish Collection, Hertfordshire Archives and Local Studies

Grace's Guide to British Industrial History, https://www.gracesguide.co.uk

Hertfordshire Archives and Local Studies (HALS), two folders containing
    information on the Rye House and the Rye House Plot
Hertfordshire Countryside, magazine
Higginbotham, P., 'The Workhouse: The Story of an Institution', website,
    http://workhouses.org.uk
historyofparliamentonline.org
lexilogos.com
Stanstead Abbots Local History Society (SALHS)

Acknowledgements for images used in this book

Most of the images in this book are photographs taken by the author, Phil Holland,
or images licensed from The Image Collection, Hertfordshire Archives and Local
Studies. In all other cases the images are either considered out of copyright or
reproduced via Creative Commons licence. While every effort has been made to
ensure no breach of copyright, please get in touch if you have any queries
regarding the images.